老子《道德經》
正解並白話對譯

Laozi's *Tao Te Ching* : The Correct Interpretation
and Translation in Vernacular Chinese

潘國鍵 著
BA, DipEd, MA, MPhil, MEd, PhD

The SenSeis

First Edition
August 2020

Published by
The SenSeis 尚尚齋
Toronto
Canada
www.thesenseis.com
publishing@thesenseis.com

ISBN 978-1-989485-17-0

目錄

潘國鍵倣八大山人山水圖　水墨紙本
53x35cm　2009年己丑

緒言

(一)

本書乃國鍵 (Kwok Kin POON) 與潘君尚 (KS Vincent POON) 合譯《An English Translation and the Correct Interpretation of Laozi's Tao Te Ching 英譯並正解老子道德經》(Toronto: The SenSeis 尚尚齋, 2020) 之後續, 同是為了正確解讀《道德經》而作。

譯句條目, 與上述英譯之書全然一致。雖則其中一兩小句, 釋義頗有修正。

例如第112條「貞」字。檢《易經•乾卦》「元亨利貞」[(i)], 貞即「正」也[(ii)]; 復據《爾雅•釋詁》「正, 長也」[(iii)]。則「貞」當解作「君長」矣。

第176條「知」字。檢《易經•繫辭》「乾知大始」[(iv)]; 又《左傳•襄公二十六年》「公孫揮曰 : 子產其將知政矣」[(v)]。遂知此「知」字義可為「主」, 解作「掌管」才更妥當。

第185條「古」字。檢《爾雅郭注》「古, 故也」[(vi)]; 而「故」者, 事理法則也。《易經•繫辭》:「仰以觀於天文, 俯以察於地理, 是故知幽明之故」[(vii)]是也。「古」字可作「事理」「法則」解, 自非毫無根據。如是, 則此條「天古」一詞, 指的當是「大自然的法則」了。

至於註釋方面, 則完整轉錄上述英譯一書Footnotes, 以作參考。引用書目亦然, 惟畧有增補。

(二)

前人之讀《道德經》, 大毛病有四:

其一, 是錯用道教的觀點來解釋。於是乎, 從來沒有超自然力量鬼神之談的《道德經》, 它裡面極之少見的「鬼」「神」兩字, 竟給說成是道教有法力的神神鬼鬼。

此外, 老子的「無欲」與道教的「無欲」, 本又截然不同。道教叫人斷絕物欲, 修道乃可成仙。老子祇勸人摒棄私欲, 依道便得無憂。事實上,《道德經》也從沒完全否定欲。它祇說「少私寡欲」

(第58條)。老子自己「欲不欲」(第175條), 不就是他的欲望麼?

二千多年來, 道教對《道德經》的抄寫和詮釋影響極大, 且大多奉之為圭臬。例如相傳生活於公元前二世紀的道士「河上公」, 乃其代表人物。

(三)

其二, 是誤以儒學的概念來解讀。於是乎, 《道德經》裡面的「仁」、「慈」、「善」、「德」等字, 全都成了儒學的那一套。這和老子思想, 當然是風馬牛不相及。

譬如說, 《道德經》既強調「天地不仁」「聖人不仁」(第13條), 何來「疏而不失」(第197條)會是獎善懲惡? 何來「報怨以德」(第170條)會是用仁德來回報仇怨? 何來「慈」會是慈愛? 且更是老子三寶之一(第182條)? 老子所推許的聖人「德善」「德信」(第134-135條), 何來解作善德、信德, 忽地全變成是孔門的德行? 老子聞之, 必然失笑! 殊不知在老子的「道」裡面, 固無所謂仁義, 更無所謂慈愛、善良和德行, 且正正還是他最嗤之以鼻的(見第三十八章)。

公元三世紀以注釋《道德經》而垂名的清談之士王弼, 竟也沒能完全擺得脫這儒學的影響。

(四)

其三, 是錯解字義, 特別是《道德經》的「若」「似」「或」三字。前人多將之解作「像似」「似乎」「或許」。因而把老子描黑為口是心非, 喜歡掩飾自己的老謀深算的思想家。事實是, 老子直斥孔子「亂人之性」[viii], 他在《道德經》裡面的言辭, 也是斬釘截鐵, 信心十足。他又怎會用上一大堆與他率直性格不合而又語意含糊的文字呢?

根據古籍, (1)「若」可解作「乃」。《說文解字注》謂「若, 又假借爲乃」[ix] 是也。故《國語•周語》云「必有忍也, 若能有濟也」[x]。(2)「似」呢, 朱駿聲、俞樾皆謂古「似」「以」相通[xi]。檢《易經•彖辭》「箕子以之」[xii], 又《漢書•高帝紀上》「鄉者夫人兒子皆以君」[xiii], 「以」皆即「似」也。而此「以」復可釋為「其」。例如《漢書•酷吏傳》稱尹齊「事張湯, 湯素稱以為廉」^(xiv)是也。(3) 至於「或」字, 則大可釋之為「常」。《論語•子路》「不恒其德, 或承之羞」^(xv)是也。

據此, 則《道德經》「似或存」(第11條)一句, 實不應解作「或似存在」, 而該釋做「其(道)常存在」。如是,《道德經》之思路文理, 始更暢順焉。論理, 道之永存, 老子必甚肯定。若然「或許」, 那《道德經》他寫來幹啥?

(五)

其四, 是上述的三種大毛病, 合起來成為二千多年來人們對《道德經》誤解、錯解、強解、曲解的更大毛病。讀之每覺老子是如斯前言不對後語, 矛盾多之又多。例如一邊勸人回返真樸, 不要私心, 卻一邊又叫人知而扮作不知, 才屬上等 (「知不知, 上」, 第192條), 十分虛偽; 既言常道無善惡, 後來卻又說天道常會幫助好人(「常與善人」, 第213條), 等等。結果, 原來道理相當簡單顯淺的《道德經》, 從此就有意無意地給扭曲成為一部難以完全理解的怪奇作品。真替老子難過!

二零二零年八月眇人潘國鍵識於多倫多如心齋。暑氣仍盛, 心卻清靜。

(i) 《易經》乾卦。鄭州: 中州古籍出版社, 1993, p.1。

(ii) 仝上, 注釋(2)引《周易正義》, 「貞, 正也」。p.2。

(iii) 郭璞, 《爾雅郭注》卷一, 釋詁下, 頁十七上。台北: 新興書局, 1964, p.011。

(iv) 《易經》繫辭上。見上, p.223。

(v) 見《康熙字典》。上海: 上海書店, 1985, p.913。

(vi) 郭璞, 《爾雅郭注》卷一, 釋詁下, 頁十一上。見上, p.008。

(vii) 《易經》繫辭上。見上, p.225。

(viii) 劉文典, 《莊子補正》, 外篇天道。雲南: 雲南人民出版社, 1980, p. 441。

(ix) 段玉裁, 《說文解字注》, 一篇下, 頁四十五上。臺北: 藝文印書館, 1966, p.44。

(x) 見《康熙字典》。見上, p.1140。

(xi) 見臺灣中央研究院, 《搜詞尋字》, 「似」(7)。

(xii) 《易經》彖辭下, 明夷卦。見上, p.130。

(xiii) 班固, 《漢書》卷一上, 高帝紀上。 香港: 中華書局, 1970, p.5。

(xiv) 班固, 《漢書》卷九十, 酷吏傳, 尹齊。見上, p. 3659。

(xv) 朱熹, 《四書集註》論語卷七, 子路。香港: 太平書局 , 1968, p. 92。

草書　137x34cm 2000AD
錄自《潘國鍵書法集》

老子《道德經》正解並白話對譯

潘國鍵 著

第一章 註釋 (1) – (7)

1. 道可道, 非常道; 名可名, 非常名。無名天地之始, 有名萬物之母。

「道」若可以用言語來解說, 就已不再是那永存不變的「道」(「常道」); 「名」若可以取名來描述, 就已不再是那永存不變的「名」(「常名」)。「無名」(「道」), 是天地宇宙的本始;「有名」(「德」), 是天下萬物的根源。

2. 故常無, 欲以觀其妙; 常有, 欲以觀其徼。

故此, 姑且用這個「常道」和「無名」, 希望能夠探索一下道的玄奧深妙; 也姑且用這個「常名」和「有名」, 希望能夠觀察一下德的萬物規迹。

3. 此兩者, 同出而異名, 同謂之玄。玄之又玄, 衆妙之門。

「無名」「有名」兩者, 雖同出於道而名稱不同, 卻同稱之為玄。玄之又玄, 它是探索「道」「德」一切奧妙至理的要門。

第二章 註釋 (8) – (15)

4. 天下皆知美之為美, 斯惡已; 皆知善之為善, 斯不善已。

天下的人都知道美的是美, 這就必有所謂醜惡了; 都知道善的是善, 這就必有所謂不善了。

5. 故有無相生, 難易相成; 長短相較, 高下相傾; 音聲相和, 前後相隨。

故此, 有和無乃相互產生, 難與易是相互變成; 長和短乃相互比較, 高與下則相互對立; 音和聲乃相互應和, 前與後則相互依存。

6. 是以聖人處無為之事, 行不言之教。 萬物作焉而不辭。 生而不有,為而不恃, 功成而弗居。 夫唯弗居, 是以不去。

所以, 依道的聖人祇擔任不為私欲而做的事情, 實踐不需言語的教化。萬物的產生和培育, 道從來不需一言。道全無實質而獨自產生, 毫不依仗而獨自作為, 事功完成也不自己居功。由於不居功, 所以這個功就永遠不會離它而去。

第三章

7. 不尚賢, 使民不爭; 不貴難得之貨, 使民不為盜; 不見可欲, 使民心不亂。

不尊崇有才能的人, 讓民眾不彼此較量; 不珍惜難得的貨物, 讓民眾不淪為盜賊; 不展示可以引起欲望的事物, 讓民眾的心緒不致煩亂。

8. 是以聖人之治, 虛其心, 實其腹, 弱其志, 強其骨。

故此聖人的治理民眾, 乃是空虛他們的內心, 充實他們的肚子, 削弱他們的意念, 健強他們的筋骨。

9. 常使民無知無欲, 使夫智者不敢為也。 為無為, 則無不治。

常常使民眾沒有知識沒有私欲, 讓那有才智的人不敢有所作為。大家做的都是不為私欲而做的事, 那民眾就沒有不治理好的了。

第四章 註釋 (16) – (21)

10. 道沖而用之或不盈。 淵兮似萬物之宗!

道乃空虛, 所以應用它常常不會盈滿。很深邃啊! 它是萬物的歸宿和根本!

11. 挫其銳, 解其紛; 和其光, 同其塵。 湛兮似或存!

頓折那鋒芒的, 消除那紛亂的; 調和那光耀的, 混同那塵垢的。很深厚啊! 它是常常存在的!

12. 吾不知誰之子，象帝之先。

我不知曉道是誰所生的，猜想是天出現前便已存在吧。

第五章 註釋 (22) – (28)

13. 天地不仁，以萬物為芻狗；聖人不仁，以百姓為芻狗。

宇宙並沒有仁愛，它把萬物當作草狗；聖人也沒有仁愛，他把民眾同樣當作草狗。

14. 天地之間，其猶橐籥乎？虛而不屈，動而愈出。

宇宙的內裡，可極似風箱麼？內裡空虛，然用之而不竭；愈拉動它呢，風就愈發吹出來了。

15. 多言數窮，不如守中。

太多說話終會辭窮，倒不如保持虛靜。

第六章 註釋 (29) – (31)

16. 谷神不死，是謂玄牝。

「谷神」(空虛的精神，道)永遠不死，這叫做道的「玄牝」(玄妙雌柔的產道)。

17. 玄牝之門，是謂天地根。

「玄牝」(玄妙雌柔的產道)閥門的開開闔闔(德)，這叫做宇宙一切的根源。

18. 緜緜若存，用之不勤。

這不斷開闔的閥門是存在的，且用它而不會竭盡。

第七章 註釋 (32) – (32)

19. 天長地久。天地所以能長且久者，以其不自生，故能長生。

宇宙長久。宇宙之所以能夠長久，因為它並不為了自己而生存，故此能夠長久生存。

20. 是以聖人後其身而身先, 外其身而身存。

所以, 聖人自己先跟隨後面, 然後自己才可以走在前面; 先拋棄自身, 然後自身才可以得到保全。

21. 非以其無私耶? 故能成其私!

這不正因為他沒有私我嗎? 故此才能夠成全他的私我呀!

第八章 註釋 (33) – (42)

22. 上善若水。水善利萬物而不爭, 處眾人之所惡, 故幾於道。

最喜好道的是水。水喜好有利萬物而不與萬物相爭, 常居於眾人所最厭惡的卑下地方, 故此它最近乎道。

23. 居善地; 心善淵; 與善仁; 言善信; 正善治; 事善能; 動善時。

身住在喜好道的地方; 心宿在喜好道的靜淵; 結交喜好道的人們; 說話則喜好本於道的誠信; 治理則喜好本於道的原則; 任用那喜好道的人才; 行動則喜好合乎道的時間。

24. 夫唯不爭, 故無尤。

因為不與人爭, 故此人們就不怨恨你了。

第九章 註釋 (43) – (49)

25. 持而盈之, 不如其已; 揣而梲之, 不可長保。

死握所有而為之滿足, 倒不如把它丟棄; 捶打東西而讓它銳利, 銳利不可能保持長久。

26. 金玉滿堂, 莫之能守; 富貴而驕, 自遺其咎。

滿屋黃金寶玉, 不能永遠保有; 富貴而放縱, 祇會留給自己災禍。

27. 功遂身退, 天之道。

功成之後自己退隱, 這才是大自然之道哩。

第十章 註釋 (50) – (68)

28. 載營魄抱一, 能無離乎？ 專氣致柔, 能嬰兒乎？ 滌除玄覽, 能無疵乎？

抱持「一」(道)來安頓自己的魂魄, 能不兩者(「一」和魂)先已分離嗎？ 抱守真氣致使柔軟, 你可及得上嬰兒嗎？ 洗淨心鏡, 能不心裏先有瑕疵嗎？

29. 愛民治國, 能無知乎？ 天門開闔, 能無雌乎？ 明白四達, 能無為乎？

愛護百姓治理國家, 能不自己運用才智嗎？ 大自然陰柔產道閥門開開闔闔, 能不自己視它做你的陰柔產道嗎？ 明白道理通達四方, 能不自己先學習知識嗎？

30. 生之, 畜之。生而不有; 為而不恃; 長而不宰。是謂玄德。

道產生一切, 養育一切。它是全無實質而獨自產生; 毫不依仗而獨自作為; 掌管一切卻又不會主宰。這叫做道的「玄德」(玄妙的德)。

第十一章 註釋 (69) – (72)

31. 三十輻, 共一轂。當其無, 有車之用。

三十條直木(輻)同組合在車輪中心的一個木圓圈(轂)。在圓圈內裡空無的地方讓車輪可以轉動, 車子才具有實用。

32. 埏埴以為器。當其無, 有器之用。

用陶泥來製成器皿。在皿內空無的地方可放置物品, 器皿才具有實用。

33. 鑿戶牖以為室。當其無, 有室之用。

鑿置門窗以成為房子。在它內裡空無的地方讓人居住, 房子才具有實用。

34. 故有之以為利, 無之以為用。

故此, 實有僅是利便, 空無才成實用。

第十二章 註釋 (73) – (76)

35. 五色令人目盲; 五音令人耳聾;
雜多的色彩讓人眼盲; 雜多的樂音讓人耳聾;

36. 五味令人口爽; 馳騁畋獵, 令人心發狂; 難得之貨, 令人行妨。
雜多的味道讓人失去辨味的能力; 馬上奔馳熱衷打獵, 讓人內心狂放; 難得的金玉財物, 使人做出損害別人的行為。

37. 是以聖人為腹不為目。故去彼取此。
所以, 聖人祇為腹飽而不為目娛。故此他丟棄那享樂的而選取這樸實的。

第十三章 註釋 (77) – (81)

38. 寵辱若驚。貴大患若身。
榮寵和羞辱都是令人惶恐的。人們亦重視大禍, 把它看成是自己的身體。

39. 何謂寵辱若驚？寵為下。得之若驚, 失之若驚。是謂寵辱若驚。
什麼叫做榮寵和羞辱乃都令人惶恐的呢? 因為尊尚的榮寵總必成為卑下的羞辱。所以, 得了榮寵乃惶恐, 這和失去榮寵是惶恐一樣。這就叫做榮寵和羞辱都是令人惶恐的了。

40. 何謂貴大患若身？吾所以有大患者, 為吾有身。及吾無身, 吾有何患？
什麼叫做重視大禍, 把它看成是自己的身體呢? 我之所以有大禍, 是因為我有著這身體呀! 假若我沒這身體, 我何來會有什麼禍患呢?

41. 故貴以身為天下, 若可寄天下; 愛以身為天下, 若可託天下。
故此, 把你重視身體化作重視天下, 天下就可以託付於你了; 把你愛惜身體化作愛惜天下, 天下就可以交託給你了。

第十四章 註釋 (82) – (94)

42. 視之不見, 名曰夷; 聽之不聞, 名曰希; 搏之不得, 名曰微。

看它而看不見, 名叫做「夷」(大); 聽它而聽不見, 名叫做「希」(靜); 執它而執不著, 名叫做「微」(無物)。

43. 此三者不可致詰, 故混而為一。其上不皦, 其下不昧。繩繩不可名, 復歸於無物。

這三者皆不可以窮究探索, 故此可混合而為一。它上面不亮白, 下面不昏污。相續不絕而無可取名, 也終必返回無物的狀態。

44. 是謂無狀之狀, 無物之象。是謂惚恍。迎之不見其首, 隨之不見其後。

這叫做沒有形狀的形狀, 沒有物象的物象。這叫做隱約不清、若有若無。迎頭看不見它的前面, 隨尾看不見它的後面。

45. 執古之道, 以御今之有。能知古始, 是謂道紀。

拿著這遠古的道, 來治理今日的州域。能夠明白這遠古的源始, 就叫做明白了道的規律。

第十五章 Chapter 15 註釋 (95) – (109)

46. 古之善為士者, 微妙玄通, 深不可識。夫唯不可識, 故強為之容:

自古以來, 喜好依道行事的人 (士, 人也), 幽深超凡, 通達大自然, 深藏而不可以認識。因為深藏而不可以認識, 故此祇能勉強把他描述一下:

47. 豫焉若冬涉川; 猶兮若畏四鄰; 儼兮其若容; 渙兮若冰之將釋; 敦兮其若樸; 曠兮其若谷; 混兮其若濁。

遲疑呀, 是冬天的徒步走過冰川; 猶疑啊, 是敬畏著四方; 恭敬啊, 他是這麼的面容莊重; 消解啊, 是冰雪的剛剛融化; 敦厚啊, 他是這麼的樸素; 遼濶啊, 他是個寬廣的山谷; 混沌啊, 他又是這麼的混濁。

48. 孰能濁以靜之徐清？孰能安以久動之徐生？保此道者，不欲盈。夫唯不盈，故能蔽不新成。

誰能夠用靜就令混濁得以漸漸清澈？誰能夠用長久震動則使安靜得以漸漸產生?(唯有道!) 知曉這道理的人，不愛自滿。因為不自滿，故此才能夠隱藏自己，決不會說親自成就了些什麼。

第十六章 註釋 (110) – (116)

49. 致虛極，守靜篤。萬物並作，吾以觀復。夫物芸芸，各復歸其根。

達到空虛至極，保持清靜專注。萬物一起產生，我憑藉它們來觀察它們的復返。事物種種，皆各自返回自己的本根(道) 。

50. 歸根曰靜，是謂復命。復命曰常，知常曰明。不知常，妄作凶。

返回本根叫做清靜，這也叫做復返大自然的運命。復返大自然運命叫做常道(不變的道)，明白常道叫做啓悟。沒明白常道，胡亂做事，那便災禍了。

51. 知常容。容乃公；公乃王；王乃天；天乃道；道乃久。沒身不殆。

明白常道，便會容納一切。容納一切乃就大公無私；大公無私乃就萬物所歸往；萬物所歸往乃就遵循於大自然；遵循於大自然乃就依循於道；依循於道乃就恆久。一輩子便不會危殆了。

第十七章 註釋 (117) – (121)

52. 太上，下知有之；其次，親而譽之；其次，畏之；其次，侮之。

最好的君主，是下面的百姓僅知他的存在(而不知他在統治); 其次的，是百姓都親近他和讚美他；再其次的，是百姓都畏懼他；再其次的，是百姓都輕蔑他。

53. 信不足？焉有不信焉! 悠兮，其貴言。

不足信麼？又豈會有不足信的哩! 憂思啊，君主當要重視他們的命令和說話呀。

54. 功成事遂, 百姓皆謂我自然。

功業有所成就, 百姓都說此乃出於我們道的本然。

第十八章 註釋 (122) – (126)

55. 大道廢, 有仁義; 慧智出, 有大偽;

大道廢棄, 才會有仁義; 聰慧機智出現, 才會有大欺詐、大虛假;

56. 六親不和, 有孝慈; 國家昏亂, 有忠臣。

六親不睦, 才會有孝慈; 國家混亂, 才會有忠臣。

第十九章 註釋 (127) – (134)

57. 絕聖棄智, 民利百倍; 絕仁棄義, 民復孝慈; 絕巧棄利, 盜賊無有。

斷絕聖賢規範, 摒棄知識才智, 民眾自會有利百倍; 斷絕仁愛, 摒棄義理, 民眾自會恢復子孝父慈; 斷絕浮偽, 摒棄貪愛, 社會就沒有盜賊了。

58. 此三者以為文不足, 故令有所屬: 見素抱樸, 少私寡欲。

上面這三個觀點由於論述的言辭未算足夠, 故此讓我再有所撰: 了解本性而抱持真樸, 少點自我而捨棄私欲。

第二十章 註釋 (135) – (155)

59. 絕學無憂。唯之與阿, 相去幾何? 善之與惡, 相去若何? 人之所畏, 不可不畏!

斷絕學習就沒憂愁了。滿意而速答的「唯」一聲, 這和不滿而緩答的「阿」一聲, 兩者相距有多少呢? 善和惡, 兩者相差有多少呢? 然而, 人們所敬畏的, 你卻不可以不敬畏呀!

60. 荒兮其未央哉! 衆人熙熙, 如享太牢, 如春登臺。我獨泊兮其未兆, 如嬰兒之未孩。儽儽兮若無所歸!

空虛啊, 它是無盡的哩! 衆人熱熱鬧鬧, 好像享受著那祭祀的祭肉; 也好像在春日登上那觀景的高臺。我卻獨自淡泊恬靜啊, 自己還未顯現; 也好像剛出生的嬰兒, 還未懂笑。懶懶懈懈啊, 我是沒有想去的地方!

61. 眾人皆有餘, 而我獨若遺。我愚人之心也哉！沌沌兮, 俗人昭昭, 我獨昏昏; 俗人察察, 我獨悶悶。

眾人都有盈餘, 祇有我獨自是丟失。我這愚昧的人的心呀! 是這麼的愚昧無知啊, 一般人清楚精明, 我獨自糊糊塗塗; 一般人析微察異, 我獨自渾渾噩噩。

62. 澹兮其若海, 飂兮若無止。眾人皆有以, 而我獨頑似鄙。我獨異於人, 而貴食母。

恬靜啊, 我是平靜的大海; 強風啊, 我是無所拘束。眾人皆有個原因, 祇有我獨自粗鈍兼鄙陋。我獨自不同於人, 祇崇尚生我育我的大自然。

第二十一章 註釋 (156) – (169)

63. 孔德之容, 惟道是從。道之為物, 惟恍惟惚。惚兮恍兮, 其中有象; 恍兮惚兮, 其中有物; 窈兮冥兮, 其中有精。

廣大空闊的德的法則, 祇會依從於道。道之成為物, 是隱約不清, 是若有若無。隱約不清啊, 若有若無啊, 它裡面有個象; 若有若無啊, 隱約不清啊, 它裡面有個物; 深遠渺茫啊, 它裡面有真氣。

64. 其精甚真, 其中有信。自古及今, 其名不去, 以閱眾甫。

它(德) 的真氣甚是純正不假, 它裏面有的是可以驗證的誠信。從古至今, 這德從沒離開過, 是靠它來賦與萬物的開始生長。

65. 吾何以知眾甫之狀哉？以此。

我怎曉得這萬物開始生長的來由呢? 是因為這個道理。

第二十二章 註釋 (170) – (179)

66. 曲則全, 枉則直; 窪則盈, 敝則新; 少則得, 多則惑。是以聖人抱一為天下式。

曲從於道就使人保全性命, 彎曲就使它伸直; 凹陷就使它盈滿, 破舊就使它變新; 缺少就使他得到, 太多就使人迷亂。故此聖人祇抱持「一」(道)來作為天下的法則。

67. 不自見, 故明; 不自是, 故彰; 不自伐, 故有功; 不自矜, 故長。
不自我炫耀, 因而得著啓悟; 不自以為是, 因而得著表彰; 不自夸功勞, 因而得保功績; 不自以為了不起, 因而得著成長做官長。

68. 夫唯不爭, 故天下莫能與之爭。古之所謂曲則全者, 豈虛言哉! 誠全而歸之。
因為他不和人相爭, 故此天下的人就沒能和他爭了。古人所說曲從於道就可以使人保全性命, 又怎會是空話呢! 這保全性命實在祇屬於他的哩。

第二十三章 註釋 (180) – (183)

69. 希言自然。故飄風不終朝, 驟雨不終日。孰為此者? 天地。天地尚不能久, 而況於人乎!
道本然的語聲, 是聽之而聽不見的清靜。故此暴風聲不會整天, 驟雨聲不會整日。誰造此風聲雨聲呢? 是宇宙。宇宙尚且不能持久, 又何況是人呢!

70. 故從事於道者: 道者同於道; 德者同於德; 失者同於失。
所以, 在追隨和尊奉於道的人來說: 追隨和尊奉於道的, 他的言行就相同於道; 追隨和尊奉於德的, 他的言行就相同於德; 喪失道和德的, 他的言行就相同於失道和失德。

71. 同於道者, 道亦樂得之; 同於德者, 德亦樂得之; 同於失者, 失亦樂得之。信不足? 焉有不信焉!
那言行相同於道的, 道也樂於以道來投合他; 那言行相同於德的, 德也樂於以德來投合他; 那喪失道和德的, 失道失德也樂於以失道失德來投合他。不足信麼? 又豈會有不足信的哩!

第二十四章 註釋 (184) – (193)

72. 企者不立, 跨者不行; 自見者不明, 自是者不彰; 自伐者無功, 自矜者不長。

提起腳跟的沒法站穩; 蹲坐著的沒能行走; 自我炫耀的無以啓悟; 自以為是的不獲表彰; 自夸功勞的沒有功績; 自以為了不起的, 不足以成長做官長。

73. 其在道也, 曰餘食贅行。物或惡之, 故有道者不處。

這等態度在道裏面呢, 叫做殘羹穢臭與贅疣醜形。這都是人們常厭惡的, 故有道的人必不會處身其中。

第二十五章 註釋 (194) – (207)

74. 有物混成, 先天地生。寂兮寥兮, 獨立不改。周行而不殆, 可以為天下母。

有種東西本然形成, 渾然一體, 在宇宙開始前便已產生。恬靜啊, 空虛啊, 獨立存在而永不改變, 循環運行而永不疲乏。它可以顯現而成為天下一切的根源(德)。

75. 吾不知其名, 字之曰道, 強為之名曰大。大曰逝; 逝曰遠; 遠曰反。故道大, 天大, 地大, 王亦大。

我不知道它的名稱, 尊稱它叫「道」, 勉強給它名號叫「大」。「大」, 於是無所不至; 無所不至, 於是極其遼遠; 極其遼遠, 於是回返於「道」。故此, 道是大, 大自然是大, 地是大, 天下所歸往的也是大。

76. 域中有四大, 而王居其一焉。人法地; 地法天; 天法道; 道法自然。

在人居處的地方裏面, 有四個大, 而天下所歸往的佔其一。人取法於地; 地取法於大自然; 大自然取法於道; 道取法於它自己的本然。

第二十六章 註釋 (208) – (215)

77. 重為輕根，靜為躁君。是以聖人終日行不離輜重。雖有榮觀，燕處超然。

重是輕的根基，靜是躁的主宰。故此聖人外遊時，笨重的行裝物資整天不會離身(寧願走慢些)。雖然享有榮譽，抱的也祇會是閑居而超脫世俗的恬靜心態。

78. 奈何萬乘之主，而以身輕天下？輕則失本，躁則失君。

因何強大國家的君主，祇為了自身而輕視天下呢？輕視天下，那就失去根基；心浮氣躁，那就失掉君位。

第二十七章 註釋 (216) – (225)

79. 善行無轍迹；善言無瑕讁；善數不用籌策；善閉無關楗而不可開；善結無繩約而不可解。

依循道的行為，沒有痕迹；依循道的說話，沒有過失；依循道的計數，不需要使用點數的細竹枝；依循道的關門，不需要使用木閂而門不可以打開；依循道的綑縛，不需要使用繩索捆綁而束縛不可以鬆解。

80. 是以聖人常善救人，故無棄人；常善救物，故無棄物。是謂襲明。

故此，聖人喜好依循常道來幫助人，本就不會嫌棄任何人；也喜好依循常道來幫忙做事，本就不會厭棄任何事物。這叫做「襲明」(獲得啟悟)。

81. 故善人者，不善人之師；不善人者，善人之資。

故此，喜好道的人，是不喜好道的人的老師；不喜好道的人，是喜好道的人的反省材料。

82. 不貴其師，不愛其資，雖智大迷。是謂要妙。

不重視自己的老師，不愛惜自己的反省材料，雖則聰智，亦是至大的迷失。這叫做「要妙」(道的精深微妙)。

第二十八章 註釋 (226) – (237)

83. 知其雄, 守其雌, 為天下谿。為天下谿, 常德不離, 復歸於嬰兒。知其白, 守其黑, 為天下式。

明白了自己的雄剛, 保持著自己的雌柔, 成為天下一切所歸往的最卑下的谿谷。能夠成為天下一切所歸往的最卑下的谿谷, 那常道的德就必不會離你而去, 於是你便返回初生嬰兒真樸的狀態了。明白這常德的清白, 保持這常德的濁黑, 用來作為天下的法則。

84. 為天下式, 常德不忒, 復歸於無極。知其榮, 守其辱, 為天下谷。為天下谷, 常德乃足, 復歸於樸。

取得天下的法則, 常德又不失誤, 就能返回道的無盡無邊。明白自己的榮寵, 保持自己的羞辱, 成為天下一切所歸往的最卑下的谿谷。成為天下一切所歸往的最卑下的谿谷, 你就完全達至常德的境界, 返回道的真樸了。

85. 樸散則為器。聖人用之, 則為官長。故大制不割。

道的真樸散發就成為各類事物。聖人治理它們, 而成為官長。正因此, 聖人亦祇會以道治理天下, 視一切無所差異。

第二十九章 註釋 (238) – (255)

86. 將欲取天下而為之, 吾見其不得已。天下神器, 不可為也。為者敗之, 執者失之。

想要獲取天下而治理它, 我看他是無法得到成功的。天下這無形無方合成的神物, 是不可以治理的。治理它的, 祇會敗壞它; 死拿著它的, 也祇會失掉它。

87. 故物或行或隨; 或歔或吹; 或強或羸; 或挫或隳。

畢竟在人裏面, 有些剛健, 有些溫順; 有些慣以鼻呼氣, 有些慣以口呼氣; 有些強壯, 有些羸弱; 有些挫服於道而自全, 有些不服於道而自毀。

88. 是以聖人去甚, 去奢, 去泰。

故此聖人丟掉溺好, 丟掉自誇, 丟掉驕縱。

第三十章 註釋 (256) – (263)

89. 以道佐人主者, 不以兵強天下。其事好還。師之所處, 荆棘生焉。大軍之後, 必有凶年。

用道來輔助君主的人, 不會以武力來鎮壓天下。武力這事情總愛招來反彈。軍旅所到的地方, 農田荒廢, 荆棘就生長了。重大的軍事行動過後, 有的必是饑荒的年歲。

90. 善有果而已, 不敢以取強。果而勿矜; 果而勿伐; 果而勿驕; 果而不得已; 果而勿強。

所以, 用兵祇喜好有個好結果罷了, 不敢採取武力來鎮壓。有好結果而不會認為了得; 有好結果而不會夸耀功績; 有好結果而不會引以為傲; 有好結果而屬無可奈何; 有好結果而非來自暴力。

91. 物壯則老, 是謂不道。不道早已!

人若壯猛則必自衰弱, 這叫不依循道。不依循道, 早就完蛋啦!

第三十一章 註釋 (264) – (275)

92. 夫佳兵者, 不祥之器。物或惡之, 故有道者不處。君子居則貴左, 用兵則貴右。兵者不祥之器, 非君子之器, 不得已而用之。恬淡為上。

最佳的軍隊呢, 也不過是不吉利的工具。人們常常厭惡它, 故此循道的人絕不處身其中。君主(君子, 君主也)在太平居閑時, 就以左邊(吉)為高; 在戰亂動兵時, 則以右邊(凶)為重。軍隊是不吉利的工具, 並非君主治國的工具, 要在無可奈何的時候才會動用它。清靜澹泊才是至上哩。

93. 勝而不美, 而美之者, 是樂殺人。夫樂殺人者, 則不可以得志於天下矣。

戰勝而不視它為快事。而視它為快事的, 便是樂於殺人了。樂於殺人, 就不可以達到自己安定天下的志願呀。

**94. 吉事尚左，凶事尚右。偏將軍居左，上將軍居右。言以喪禮處
之。殺人之眾，以哀悲泣之。戰勝以喪禮處之。**

在吉祥的事情上以左邊為高，在不吉利的事情上以右邊為重。所
以，軍隊的副將坐在左邊，主帥則坐在右邊。這是說用喪禮來對待
軍事了。殺人的兵眾，因為悲傷而為死者痛哭。戰爭勝利，也祇會
用喪禮來對待它。

第三十二章 註釋 (276) – (285)

**95. 道常無名樸。雖小，天下莫能臣也。侯王若能守之，萬物將自
賓。天地相合，以降甘露。民莫之令而自均。**

道是不變、無名、真樸。雖然低微，但天下卻沒有東西能臣服它
的。諸侯若能保持著它，萬物必自歸順。猶如大自然和大地彼此
配合，因而降下甘美的露水。故此百姓無需命令，也自會遵從上面
的君主了。(亦即陶均一轉，陶泥立即自動往上移。)

96. 始制有名。名亦既有，夫亦將知止。知止可以不殆。

「始」(道) 產生了「有名」(德)。「有名」(德)既已有了，便須知
曉自己所應至和所應停的地方。知曉自己所應至和所應停的地方，
就可以沒危殆了。

97. 譬道之在天下，猶川谷之於江海。

遂明白道之在於天下，猶如水川山谷之在於江海。(亦即有道才有
天下，有川谷才有江海。)

第三十三章 註釋 (286) – (292)

98. 知人者智，自知者明。勝人者有力，自勝者強。

懂得人事的，祇是才智；認識自己的，方是啓悟。制服別人的，祇是
有力氣；克制自己的，方是力量強。

99. 知足者富，強行者有志。不失其所者久，死而不亡者壽。

懂得滿足的，便是富裕；勤力實踐的，才是有志氣。不丟失道的，便
活得長久；身死而道不滅的，才是真長壽。

第三十四章 註釋 (293) – (296)

100. 大道氾兮, 其可左右。萬物恃之而生而不辭; 功成不名有; 衣養萬物而不為主。

大道氾濫啊, 它可以左右上下無所不至。萬物依仗它而產生和培育, 而它卻從來不需一言; 事功完成, 它亦從來不稱有功; 覆蓋(保護) 和養育萬物, 而它也從來不做主宰。

101. 常無欲可名於小; 萬物歸焉而不為主, 可名為大。以其終不自為大, 故能成其大。

常道沒有私欲, 可以稱它為小; 萬物都返歸道呀, 而它卻從不做主宰, 故亦可以稱它為大。正因為它永不自己成為大, 故此才能成就它的大哩。

第三十五章 註釋 (297) – (305)

102. 執大象, 天下往。往而不害, 安平太。樂與餌, 過客止。

拿著最大的物象(無形之象, 道), 天下便歸往你了。歸往你而沒了禍害, 大家從此便安享寧靜太平了。若你有的祇是悅耳的音樂和可口的糕點, 那就祇能暫且吸引過路的旅客罷了。

103. 道之出口, 淡乎其無味。視之不足見; 聽之不足聞; 用之不足既。

道若口講出來, 它是平淡而無味的。要看它呢, 你不能看得見; 要聽它呢, 你不能聽得見; 要運用它呢, 卻是用之不能竭盡的。

第三十六章 註釋 (306) – (312)

104. 將欲歙之, 必固張之; 將欲弱之, 必固強之; 將欲廢之, 必固興之; 將欲奪之, 必固與之。是謂微明。

打算收縮某物, 必先一心擴張它; 打算削弱某物, 必先一心增強它; 打算廢棄某物, 必先一心建立它; 打算爭取某物, 必先一心給它予人。這叫做「微明」(由無物而來的啟悟)。

105. 柔弱勝剛強。魚不可脫於淵。國之利器不可以示人。

柔軟勝過剛硬。活健的魚兒不可以脫離柔軟的淵水。有利治理國家的強硬工具(例如軍隊、律法等), 切不可以輕易展示人們。

第三十七章 註釋 (313) – (320)

106. 道常無為而無不為。侯王若能守之, 萬物將自化。化而欲作, 吾將鎮之以無名之樸。

道永不為私欲而作為, 所以它無所不能做。諸侯若能保持它, 萬物必自化育。化育而產生私欲, 我必用「無名」(道)的真樸來抑制它。

107. 無名之樸, 夫亦將無欲。不欲以靜, 天下將自定。

「無名」(道)的真樸, 祇是遵奉沒有私欲。沒有私欲而使人清靜, 天下自必安定。

第三十八章 註釋 (321) – (330)

108. 上德不德, 是以有德; 下德不失德, 是以無德。上德無為而無以為; 下德為之而有以為。

上等德行的人無需德行, 因此亦正顯示他本已具有德行; 下等德行的人不想失去德行, 因此反顯露他本來就是沒甚德行。上等德行的人不做修養德行的工夫, 這是沒原因去做; 下等德行的人做修養德行的工夫, 這是有原因去做。

109. 上仁為之而無以為; 上義為之而有以為。上禮為之而莫之應, 則攘臂而扔之。

尊崇仁的人做修養仁的工夫, 這是沒原因去做(天地沒有仁); 尊崇義的人做修養義的工夫, 這是有原因去做(相信有善果); 尊崇禮的人去做修養禮的工夫, 然而沒有人響應, 他就捲袖露膊, 強拉別人來遵從。

110. 故失道而後德; 失德而後仁; 失仁而後義; 失義而後禮。

故此, 丟失了道, 然後有所謂「德」(德行); 丟失了德, 然後有所謂「仁」; 丟失了仁, 然後有所謂「義」; 丟失了義, 然後有所謂「

禮」。

111. 夫禮者，忠信之薄，而亂之首。前識者，道之華，而愚之始。是以大丈夫處其厚，不居其薄；處其實，不居其華。故去彼取此。

禮，是忠誠信實的淺薄，也是擾亂人性的罪魁禍首。世上所謂有先見的人，看的祇是道外表淺薄的華美，這也是愚昧的開始。所以，有志氣於道的人，祇會住在道深厚的地方，而不會住在道淺薄的地方；他祇會置身在道內裡的實樸，而不會置身在道外表的虛華。故此丟棄那先見的淺薄愚昧，而選取這置身在道深厚的地方。

第三十九章 註釋 (331) – (343)

112. 昔之得一者：天得一以清；地得一以寧；神得一以靈；谷得一以盈；萬物得一以生；侯王得一以為天下貞。其致之。

久遠的時候，那得到了「一」(道)的：大自然得到「一」，從而清淨；大地得到「一」，從而安寧；精神得到「一」，從而美好；山谷得到「一」，從而盈滿；萬物得到「一」，從而產生；諸侯得到「一」，從而成為天下的君長。這全都是由「一」而來的。

113. 天無以清，將恐裂；地無以寧，將恐發；神無以靈，將恐歇；谷無以盈，將恐竭；萬物無以生，將恐滅；侯王無以貴高，將恐蹶。

大自然若無從清淨，它恐怕必會破裂；大地若無從安寧，它恐怕必會晃動；精神若無從美好，它恐怕必會衰竭；山谷若無從盈滿，它恐怕必會窮盡；萬物若無從產生，它恐怕必會絕滅；諸侯若無從高貴，他恐怕必會給人顛覆。

114. 故貴以賤為本，高以下為基。是以侯王自稱孤、寡、不穀。此非以賤為本邪？非乎？故致數輿無輿。不欲琭琭如玉，珞珞如石。

故此，尊貴實以卑賤為根本，高上實以低下為基礎。此所以諸侯自稱「孤」、「寡」、「不穀」(不善)。這不正是以低賤為根本嗎？可不是麼？故此，那些擁有數馬拉動車子的王侯公卿的高貴，本就是建築在連車子也沒有的貧困平民的低賤之上。他們當不想自己耀目如珍貴的寶玉，顯眼如頸上項鏈的寶石。

第四十章 註釋 (344) – (346)

115. 反者道之動; 弱者道之用。天下萬物生於有, 有生於無。

使一切復返於道, 這是道的行動; 柔軟空虛, 這是道的應用。天下萬物產生於「有」(有名, 德), 「有」來自於「無」(無名, 道)。

第四十一章 註釋 (347) – (366)

116. 上士聞道, 勤而行之; 中士聞道, 若存若亡; 下士聞道, 大笑之。不笑不足以為道。

上等的人聽見道, 勤奮地實踐它; 中等的人聽見道, 有時保存有時失去; 下等的人聽見道, 捧腹大笑它。不捧腹大笑呢, 它就不足以成為道了。

117. 故建言有之 : 明道若昧; 進道若退; 夷道若纇; 上德若谷; 大白若辱; 廣德若不足; 建德若偷; 質真若渝; 大方無隅; 大器晚成; 大音希聲; 大象無形; 道隱無名。

故此古語有句說話: 昭明的道乃是昏蒙; 前進的道乃是後退; 坦平的道乃是不平; 最高的德乃是低谷; 最清白的德乃是污濁; 最寬廣的德乃是不夠; 最健厚的德乃是脆薄; 最樸素的純正乃是變污; 最大的矩形沒有角; 最大的事物需長時間來完成; 最大的音響聽不見聲音; 最大的物象沒有形象; 所以, 道是微妙不可見而「無名」。

118. 夫唯道善貸且成。

祇有道才善於施予一切和成就一切。

第四十二章 註釋 (367) – (374)

119. 道生一; 一生二; 二生三; 三生萬物。萬物負陰而抱陽, 沖氣以為和。

道產生「一」;「一」產生「二」;「二」產生「三」;「三」產生萬物。萬物皆具有「陰」而藏有「陽」, 並由這陰陽兩氣相激盪而成和合。

120. 人之所惡, 唯孤、寡、不穀, 而王公以為稱。故物或損之而益, 或益之而損。

人們所厭惡的, 肯定是「孤」、「寡」、「不穀」(不善), 然而天子諸侯都用作自稱。故此, 事物常常是減損它卻反而增益它, 也常常是增益它卻反而減損它。

121. 人之所教, 我亦教之。強梁者不得其死, 吾將以為教父。

人們所教化的, 我也用它來教化人。「剛強橫暴的人不得善終」, 我必用它作為教化的開始。

第四十三章 註釋 (375) – (380)

122. 天下之至柔, 馳騁天下之至堅。無有入無間。吾是以知無為之有益。

天下的最柔軟, 自由地遊走在天下的最堅硬裡面。不見形相的東西, 可以滲入沒有空隙的地方。我故此懂得不為私欲而做是很有益處的。

123. 不言之教, 無為之益, 天下希及之。

不需言語而教化, 不為私欲做事而得益, 天下的人極少達得到。

第四十四章 註釋 (381) – (384)

124. 名與身孰親？身與貨孰多？得與亡孰病？是故甚愛必大費, 多藏必厚亡。

名譽和身體, 哪更深愛？身體和財物, 哪更重要？貪得和喪失, 哪更痛苦？因此, 愛惜深必然損耗大, 儲藏多必也喪失多。

125. 知足不辱; 知止不殆; 可以長久。

懂得滿足, 就不會招來羞辱; 知曉自己所應至和所應停的地方, 就可以沒危殆; 這就可以活得長久。

第四十五章 註釋 (385) – (396)

126. 大成若缺, 其用不弊; 大盈若沖, 其用不窮。大直若屈, 大巧若拙, 大辯若訥。

最大的完備乃是缺少, 它的應用不會竭盡; 最大的盈滿乃是空虛, 它的應用不會窮盡。最大的正直乃是屈折(於道); 最大的靈巧乃是遲鈍; 最大的善辯乃是笨口拙舌。

127. 躁勝寒, 靜勝熱。清靜為天下正。

疾動稍能克制寒涼, 惟清靜始可克服苦熱。清靜才是天下的正道。

第四十六章 註釋 (397) – (398)

128. 天下有道, 卻走馬以糞; 天下無道, 戎馬生於郊。

天下有了道, 良馬便返歸農地, 用作施肥耕田; 天下沒有了道, 可戰馬就養育在郊野了。

129. 禍莫大於不知足; 咎莫大於欲得。故知足之足, 常足矣!

災禍沒有大得過不懂滿足; 罪咎沒有大得過貪得無厭。故此懂得滿足而來的滿足, 才是永久的滿足呀!

第四十七章 註釋 (399) – (401)

130. 不出戶知天下, 不闚牖見天道。其出彌遠, 其知彌少。

足不出戶, 而知曉天下間的事情; 不望窗外, 而瞭解大自然的事理。人若出門愈遠, 他了解的便愈少。

131. 是以聖人不行而知, 不見而名, 不為而成。

所以聖人不需外遊而自會知曉, 不需看見而自會明白, 不為私欲做事而自會成就。

第四十八章 註釋 (402) – (406)

132. 為學日益, 為道日損。損之又損, 以至於無為。無為而無不為。

求取學識, 私欲一天一天的增加; 求取道呢, 私欲一天一天的損減。私欲損減又再損減, 結果達到不為私欲去做事。不為私欲去做事, 那就無所不能做了。

133. 取天下常以無事。及其有事, 不足以取天下。

治理天下永須憑藉不做大事。當人想去成就些什麼大事時, 他就已經沒資格去治理天下了。

第四十九章 註釋 (407) – (415)

134. 聖人無常心, 以百姓心為心。善者, 吾善之; 不善者, 吾亦善之。德善。

聖人沒有既定不變的私心, 祇以百姓的心作為自己的心。百姓喜好的, 我也喜好他們所喜好的; 百姓不喜好的, 我也喜好他們這個不喜好。這才得到與百姓完全一樣的喜(與不喜)。

135. 信者, 吾信之; 不信者, 吾亦信之。德信。

百姓信服的, 我也信服他們所信服的; 百姓不信服的, 我也信服他們這個不信服。這才得到與百姓完全一樣的信(與不信)。

136. 聖人在天下, 歙歙為天下渾其心。聖人皆孩之。

聖人在天下裡面, 了無偏執地與天下人心同返質樸。如是聖人和天下的人, 都回復嬰孩的狀態了。

第五十章 註釋 (416) – (425)

137. 出生入死, 生之徒, 十有三; 死之徒, 十有三; 人之生, 動之死地, 亦十有三。夫何故? 以其生生之厚!

從出生到死亡期間, 活著的人們 (徒, 眾也), 有四肢九竅的身軀; 死去的人們, 也有四肢九竅的身軀; 人在活著時, 每每往赴必死絕地來犯險, 亦同樣有著此四肢九竅的身軀。這是件什麼事情呢? 就是為了這身軀而令人太看重自己的財物和性命啊!

138. 蓋聞善攝生者, 陸行不遇兕虎, 入軍不被甲兵。兕無所投其角, 虎無所措其爪, 兵無所容其刃。夫何故？以其無死地。

聽說喜好養生的人, 陸上行走不會遇上兕牛(獨角青色)和老虎等猛獸, 進入軍陣也不會接觸到武裝的士兵。於是兕牛沒處撞入牠的尖角, 老虎沒處刺入牠的利爪, 士兵也沒處使用他的刀劍。這是什麼原故呢? 是因為他不會讓自己置身於必死的絕地呀!

第五十一章 註釋 (426) – (433)

139. 道生之, 德畜之; 物形之, 勢成之。是以萬物莫不尊道而貴德。

道產生了一切, 德養育了一切; 形色顯現了一切, 形態實現了一切。故此萬物無不尊崇道而崇尚德。

140. 道之尊, 德之貴, 夫莫之命而常自然。故道生之, 德畜之。長之育之; 亭之毒之; 養之覆之。生而不有, 為而不恃, 長而不宰。是謂玄德。

道受尊崇, 德受崇尚。萬物不需它們命令, 就永遠依循道的本然。畢竟是道產生了一切, 德養育了一切。它們生長一切, 培育一切; 化育一切, 長育一切; 供養一切, 最終又把一切返回於道。道是全無實質而獨自產生; 毫不依仗而獨自作為; 掌管一切卻又不會主宰。這叫道的「玄德」(玄妙的德)。

第五十二章 註釋 (434) – (443)

141. 天下有始, 以為天下母。既得其母, 以知其子; 既知其子, 復守其母, 沒身不殆

天下有個「始」(道), 它顯現而成為天下一切的根源(德)。既了解天下一切的根源, 就能夠知曉由這根源而來的一切事物; 能夠知曉由這根源而來的一切事物, 再保持著這一切事物的根源, 這便一輩子不會危殆了。

142. 塞其兌, 閉其門, 終身不勤; 開其兌, 濟其事, 終身不救。

堵塞你的耳目鼻口(聲色氣味等快感), 關閉你和外界思想接觸的門戶, 你一輩子就不會竭盡; 張開你的耳目鼻口, 成就你的大事, 那你一輩子都得不到道的幫助。

143. 見小曰明, 守柔曰強。用其光, 復歸其明, 無遺身殃。是為習常。

了解「小」(道), 叫做啓悟; 保持「柔」(德), 叫做韌強。運用道的明亮, 返回道的啓悟, 切不要留給自己災殃。這就是「習常」(瞭解常道)。

第五十三章 註釋 (444) – (451)

144. 使我介然有知, 行於大道, 唯施是畏。大道甚夷, 而民好徑。

假使我堅定不移, 對道有所瞭解, 並在此「大道」上行走, 但實行起來, 心中還是敬畏著的。大道十分平坦, 祇是民眾卻喜歡走小徑。

145. 朝甚除, 田甚蕪, 倉甚虛。服文綵, 帶利劍; 厭飲食, 財貨有餘。是謂盜夸, 非道也哉!

宮室建造太多, 田地因此十分荒蕪, 穀倉因此十分空虛。穿著華美衣服, 攜帶鋒利刀劍; 酒餚過飽, 錢物有剩。這叫做賊魁, 絕不是道呀!

第五十四章 註釋 (452) – (459)

146. 善建者不拔; 善抱者不脫。子孫以祭祀不輟。

喜好修立道的人, 不會把它拔除; 喜好抱持道的人, 不會把它脫掉。他的子孫, 因而可以代代祭祀不絕。

147. 修之於身, 其德乃真; 修之於家, 其德乃餘; 修之於鄉, 其德乃長; 修之於國, 其德乃豐; 修之於天下, 其德乃普。

為了自身而修養道, 他的德乃就真樸; 為了家庭而修養道, 他的德乃就豐足; 為了家鄉而修養道, 他的德乃就更為增長; 為了國家而修養道, 他的德乃就更為豐厚; 為了天下而修養道, 他的德乃就更為全面而普及。

148. 故以身觀身; 以家觀家; 以鄉觀鄉; 以國觀國; 以天下觀天下。吾何以知天下然哉? 以此。

故此, 為自身而修養道, 可以用它來觀察自身; 為家庭而修養道, 可以用它來觀察家庭; 為家鄉而修養道, 可以用它來觀察家鄉; 為國家而修養道, 可以用它來觀察國家; 為天下而修養道, 可以用它來觀察天下。我怎曉得天下事物是如此的呢? 就因為這個道理。

第五十五章 註釋 (460) – (479)

149. 含德之厚, 比於赤子。蜂蠆虺蛇不螫, 猛獸不據, 攫鳥不搏。骨弱筋柔而握固。

藏德的深厚, 及得上初生的嬰兒。初生嬰兒, 蜂蠆虺蛇等有毒蛇蟲不會咬他, 猛獸不會撲抓他, 兇鳥也不會拍擊他。他筋骨柔軟, 握拳卻是十分堅固。

150. 未知牝牡之合而全作, 精之至也。終日號而不嗄, 和之至也。知和曰常, 知常曰明。

嬰兒不曉得陰氣陽氣相調合, 卻能完好無損地成長, 這可說是真氣的極致了。整日號哭而不會聲音嘶啞, 這可說是陰陽和合的極致了。了解陰陽和合, 便叫懂得常道; 了解常道, 便叫得著啓悟。

151. 益生曰祥, 心使氣曰強。物壯則老, 謂之不道。不道早已。

強要添財加壽, 這叫災凶(古祥字可吉可凶); 恣逞意氣, 這叫橫暴。人若壯猛強橫, 則必自衰弱, 可稱之為不依循道。不依循道, 早就完蛋啦!

第五十六章 註釋 (480) – (482)

152. 知者不言, 言者不知。塞其兌, 閉其門; 挫其銳, 解其分; 和其光, 同其塵。是謂玄同。

明白道的人不說它出來, 說它出來的人並不明白。堵塞你的耳目鼻口(聲色氣味等快感), 關閉你和外界思想接觸的門戶; 頓折那鋒芒的, 消除那紛亂的; 調和那光耀的, 混同那塵垢的。這叫做道的

「玄同」(玄妙的合一)。

153. 故不可得而親，不可得而疏；不可得而利，不可得而害；不可得而貴，不可得而賤。故為天下貴。

故此，你沒能夠找得什麼才是親近的，也沒能夠找得什麼才是疏遠的；沒能夠找得什麼才是有利的，也沒能夠找得什麼才是有害的；沒能夠找得什麼才是地位高的，也沒能夠找得什麼才是地位低的。故此你就成為天下間最受敬重的人了。

第五十七章 註釋 (483) – (496)

154. 以正治國，以奇用兵，以無事取天下。吾何以知其然哉？以此。

治國依仗正道，用兵認為不祥，治天下憑藉不做大事。我怎曉得這該如此的呢？就因為這個道理。

155. 天下多忌諱，而民彌貧；民多利器，國家滋昏；人多伎巧，奇物滋起；法令滋彰，盜賊多有。

天下愈多顧忌，民眾便愈更貧困；民眾愈多有利自己的工具(例如貨幣)，國家便愈增混亂；人們愈多技藝，奇特事物便愈加興起；法律命令愈增彰顯，便有愈多盜賊出現。

156. 故聖人云：我無為，而民自化；我好靜，而民自正；我無事，而民自富；我無欲，而民自樸。

故此聖人說: 我不為私欲去做事，而民眾自會化育；我喜歡清靜，而民眾自會回返天下的正道；我不做大事，而民眾自會富裕；我沒有私欲，而民眾自會實樸。

第五十八章 註釋 (497) – (510)

157. 其政悶悶，其民淳淳；其政察察，其民缺缺。

君主施政渾渾噩噩，他的百姓便是淳樸篤厚；君主施政析微察異，他的百姓便去弄虛作假。

158. 禍兮福之所倚, 福兮禍之所伏。孰知其極? 其無正! 正復為奇, 善復為妖。

禍啊, 它是福所依仗的; 福啊, 它是禍所潛藏的。誰曉得這禍這福最終會是怎麼樣呢? 這實在沒有所謂美善的呀! 美的可反過來成為奇邪, 善的可反過來成為怪異。

159. 人之迷, 其日固久。是以聖人方而不割, 廉而不劌, 直而不肆, 光而不燿。

人們迷失於道, 這些日子已經很長久了。此所以聖人始能方正而視一切無所差異, 廉潔而不傷及別人, 正直而不和人衝突, 明亮而不耀眼於人。

第五十九章 註釋 (511) – (522)

160. 治人事天莫若嗇。夫唯嗇, 是謂早服。早服謂之重積德。重積德則無不克。無不克則莫知其極。

在修養自己事奉大自然的事情上, 大家就比不上農夫了。祇有農夫, 才可稱得上起初就已服從了大自然(德)。起初就已服從大自然, 乃可稱之為重視慢慢累積而得到收穫。能重視慢慢累積而得成果, 那就無所不能勝任了。無所不能勝任, 人們便不知道你能力的極限了。

161. 莫知其極, 可以有國。有國之母, 可以長久。是謂深根固柢, 長生久視之道。

人們不知道你能力的極限, 你便可以治理國家了。用德來治理國家, 那就可以長久了。這叫做根深柢固, 乃長生久活的原則和途徑。

第六十章 註釋 (523) – (528)

162. 治大國若烹小鮮。以道莅天下, 其鬼不神。非其鬼不神, 其神不傷人。非其神不傷人, 聖人亦不傷人!

治理大國有如烹煮小魚(務必留神, 切勿傷害魚身的完好)。用道來治理天下的人, 他的敏慧不會是他的精神。並不是因為他的敏慧不是他的精神, 而是他的精神不會傷害人。並不是因為他的精神不傷害人, 而是遵道的聖人確實本來就是不會傷害人啊!

163. 夫兩不相傷, 故德交歸焉。

君主和百姓互不傷害, 故得同返於道了。

第六十一章 註釋 (529) – (536)

164. 大國者下流, 天下之交, 天下之牝。牝常以靜勝牡, 以靜為下。

大國應當自處於卑下的微賤, 成為天下歸會的地方, 也成為天下間最雌柔的代表。雌柔之所以常能用它的清靜去克服雄剛, 正因清靜就是卑下。

165. 故大國以下小國, 則取小國; 小國以下大國, 則取大國。故或下以取, 或下而取。

故此, 大國若以謙下來對待小國, 則取得小國的信服; 小國以謙下來接待大國, 則取得大國的信任。所以, 他們有些憑謙下以取得信服, 有些憑謙下而取得信任。

166. 大國不過欲兼畜人, 小國不過欲入事人。夫兩者各得其所欲。大者宜為下。

大國不過想去兼并他人, 小國不過想得到采納來侍奉別人。大小兩國於是各得它們所想要的。而最重要的, 乃是彼此都應成為謙下。

第六十二章 註釋 (537) – (549)

167. 道者萬物之奧。善人之寶, 不善人之所保。美言可以市, 尊行可以加人。

道是萬物安棲的舒適地方。它是喜好道的人的寶物, 也是不喜好道的人所以安保。漂亮說話祇可以用在市集買賣, 遵道而行卻可以施益眾人。

168. 人之不善, 何棄之有? 故立天子, 置三公, 雖有拱璧以先駟馬, 不如坐進此道。

對於不喜好道的人, 道又怎會丟棄他們呢? 故此, 確立天子設置三公，雖則天子有拱璧之大的財寶，三公有駟馬之車的尊崇，倒不如自然而然地實踐此道。

169. 古之所以貴此道者何？不曰：以求得，有罪以免邪？故為天下貴。

古來所以崇尚這道，究是什麼緣故呢？不就是說「用道來求，必會得著；若有罪過，歸道即脫」麼？故此它受天下人崇尚。

第六十三章 註釋 (550) – (553)

170. 為無為；事無事；味無味。大小多少，報怨以德。

幹那沒有私欲的行為；做那沒有大功的事情；嚐那沒有好壞的味道。無分大小多少，我僅用德(大自然的規律)來回應仇怨。

171. 圖難於其易，為大於其細。天下難事，必作於易；天下大事，必作於細。

對付難題，要在它還是容易的時候；處理大事，要在它還是小事的時候。天下難事，必定始自容易；天下大事，必定始於微小。

172. 是以聖人終不為大，故能成其大。夫輕諾必寡信，多易必多難。是以聖人猶難之，故終無難矣。

此所以聖人終身不做大事，因此才能夠成就他的大。輕易許諾，必然少守信用；多麼的容易，必成多麼的困難。故此，這是個聖人尚且難以解決的問題呀！聖人不做大事，因此終身沒困難了。

第六十四章 註釋 (554) – (571)

173. 其安易持，其未兆易謀。其脆易泮，其微易散。為之於未有，治之於未亂。合抱之木，生於毫末；九層之臺，起於累土；千里之行，始於足下。

靜態的事情，易於掌握；未發生的事情，易於謀策。脆弱的事情，易於擊碎；微小的事情，易於破散。在事情還未發生前，便要預先治理；在事情還未紛亂前，便要預先整治。給人砍伐的粗如合抱的巨樹，生長自極細的幼苗；甚費人力物力的九層巨大高臺，開始於堆積第一筐的泥土；無益於道的千里外遊，開始於你提起腳掌走的第一步。

174. 為者敗之, 執者失之。是以聖人無為故無敗; 無執故無失。民之從事, 常於幾成而敗之。慎終如始, 則無敗事。

為了私欲而做事的, 祇會敗壞它; 死拿著物件的, 祇會失掉它。所以聖人不會為私欲而去做事, 因此便不會敗壞它; 他不會死拿著物件, 因此就不會失掉它。民眾做事, 常常在將要成功的時候而敗壞了它。假若做事情到了最後還能像剛開始時一樣, 謹慎遵道而不為私欲去做, 那就決不會有失敗的事情啦。

175. 是以聖人欲不欲, 不貴難得之貨。學不學, 復眾人之所過。以輔萬物之自然而不敢為。

故此, 聖人祇希望沒有私欲, 也不會重視難得的財物。他效法不去學習知識, 要讓人們復得他們所失掉的道。他祇想幫助萬物回返道的本然, 而絕不敢為私欲而行事。

第六十五章 註釋 (572) – (575)

176. 古之善為道者, 非以明民, 將以愚之。民之難治, 以其智多。故以智治國, 國之賊; 不以智治國, 國之福。知此兩者亦稽式。

自古以來喜好實踐道的人, 不會使民眾聰明, 反而要讓他們愚笨。民眾之難以治理, 是因為他們才智太多。故此, 若用才智來治理國家, 他便是破壞國家的人了。若不用才智來治理國家, 這便是國家的福氣了。而掌管這兩種不同事況的, 都是那合乎道的同一法則。

177. 常知稽式, 是謂玄德。玄德深矣, 遠矣, 與物反矣, 然後乃至大順。

常道掌管各不同事況而總合乎它的同一法則, 這叫道的「玄德」(玄妙的德)。「玄德」深厚呀, 遼遠呀, 它參與萬物同返於道呀, 然後一切乃達到「大順」(最大的順應於道)。

第六十六章 註釋 (576) – (582)

178. 江海所以能為百谷王者, 以其善下之, 故能為百谷王。

江海之所以能夠成為眾谷水流歸往的地方, 因為它喜好低於山谷,所以能夠成為眾谷水流歸往的地方。

179. 是以欲上民, 必以言下之; 欲先民, 必以身後之。

故此, 若希望居於民眾之上, 那就必須我先處於民眾之下。若希望
站在前面領導民眾, 那就必須自己先跟隨在民眾的後面。

**180. 是以聖人處上而民不重, 處前而民不害。是以天下樂推而不
厭。以其不爭, 故天下莫能與之爭。**

故此, 聖人居於高位, 而民眾不覺得他是一重負擔; 居於領導, 而民
眾也不覺得他會帶來傷害。所以, 天下的人樂意擁戴他, 而不會厭
棄他。因為他不和別人相爭, 故此天下的人就沒能和他爭了。

第六十七章 註釋 (583) – (595)

**181. 天下皆謂我道大, 似不肖。夫唯大, 故似不肖。若肖, 久矣其
細也夫!**

世人都認為我說道大, 但它卻全不似大。正因為大, 故此它才全不
似大呢。假若似大, 它老早就是細啦!

**182. 我有三寶, 持而保之: 一曰慈, 二曰儉, 三曰不敢為天下先。慈
故能勇; 儉故能廣; 不敢為天下先, 故能成器長。**

我有三寶, 常緊握而依仗著它: 一稱為篤愛於道, 二稱為節儉素樸,
三稱為不敢做天下的領導。篤愛於道, 故此能夠大有勇氣; 節儉素
樸, 故此能夠增加畜積; 不敢做天下的領導, 故此能夠成為受器重
的官長。

**183. 今舍慈且勇; 舍儉且廣; 舍後且先。死矣! 夫慈以戰則勝, 以
守則固。天將救之, 以慈衛之。**

今日人們捨棄篤愛於道而想取得勇氣; 捨棄節儉素樸而想取得畜
積; 捨棄跟隨在民眾後面而想站在前面領導民眾。這必死無疑的
呀! 人若用篤愛於道來戰鬥, 就必會取勝; 用它來防守, 就必會牢
固。大自然必會幫助他, 用他的篤愛於道來保衛他。

第六十八章 註釋 (596) – (599)

184. 善為士者, 不武; 善戰者, 不怒; 善勝敵者, 不與; 善用人者, 為之下。

善於做將帥的, 不會勇猛; 善於戰鬥的, 不會暴怒; 善於戰勝敵人的, 不會和敵人戰鬥; 善於用人的, 要做人之下。

185. 是謂不爭之德, 是謂用人之力, 是謂配天古之極。

這叫做不和人相爭的得益, 這叫做善用人才的本領, 這叫做結合大自然的法則而至於極點。

第六十九章 註釋 (600) – (608)

186. 用兵有言: 吾不敢為主, 而為客; 不敢進寸, 而退尺。

指揮戰事的人有句說話: 我不敢做主方去攻擊, 祇會做客方來防守; 不敢冒進半寸, 祇會退守一尺。

187. 是謂行無行; 攘無臂; 扔無敵; 執無兵。

這叫做前進卻看作是沒法前進; 摧毀對方卻看作是不敵對方; 拿了兵器卻看作是沒拿兵器。

188. 禍莫大於輕敵。輕敵幾喪吾寶。故抗兵相加, 哀者勝矣。

災禍沒有大得過輕敵。輕敵則失掉我的三寶。故此, 舉兵抵擋敵人, 悲慟的一方總會獲得勝利呀。

第七十章 註釋 (609) – (616)

189. 吾言甚易知, 甚易行。天下莫能知, 莫能行。

我的言論十分容易明白, 也十分容易實踐。可惜天下的人沒能明白, 也沒能實踐。

190. 言有宗, 事有君。夫唯無知, 是以不我知。

言論要有個根本, 事物總有個主宰(德)。祇因人們不懂得這個道理, 所以才不了解我。

191. 知我者希, 則我者貴。是以聖人被褐懷玉!

了解我的人極少, 效法我的更屬難能可貴。故此也證明了聖人身上穿的是卑賤的麻衣, 心內藏的卻是無價的寶玉呀!

第七十一章 註釋 (617) – (620)

192. 知不知, 上; 不知知, 病。

能知曉那些不懂道的, 此乃優尚; 沒能知曉那懂道的, 可就疲苦了。

193. 夫唯病病, 是以不病。聖人不病, 以其病病, 是以不病。

因為了解疲苦之所以成為疲苦, 所以才會不疲苦。聖人不疲苦, 因為他了解疲苦之所以成為疲苦, 所以就不疲苦了。

第七十二章 註釋 (621) – (624)

194. 民不畏威, 則大威至。無狎其所居, 無厭其所生。夫唯不厭, 是以不厭。

當百姓再不懼怕君主的威嚇時, 他們天大的怒威便即來臨了。不要遷移人們居住的地方, 也不要傷害人們維生的生計。因為你不迫害百姓, 故此百姓才不會傷害你。

195. 是以聖人自知不自見; 自愛不自貴。故去彼取此。

所以, 聖人認識自己, 但不會自我炫耀; 愛護自己, 但不會抬高自己。故此丟棄君主那妄自尊大的, 而選取這謙虛卑下的。

第七十三章 註釋 (625) – (629)

196. 勇於敢則殺; 勇於不敢則活。此兩者, 或利或害。天之所惡, 孰知其故？是以聖人猶難之!

勇於進取的那就喪命; 勇於不進取的那就活命。這兩者, 有利也有害。大自然之所厭惡, 誰曉得箇中的原故呢？所以, 這是個聖人尚且難以解決的問題呀!

197. 天之道, 不爭而善勝, 不言而善應; 不召而自來, 繟然而善謀。 天網恢恢, 疏而不失。

大自然的規律, 不相爭而善於贏取, 不說話而善於應對; 不需召喚而自己前來, 鬆緩舒坦地而善於謀劃。大自然的巨網寬闊廣大, 雖是寬闊, 但絕不會漏失任何東西。

第七十四章 註釋 (630) – (634)

198. 民不畏死, 奈何以死懼之? 若使民常畏死而為奇者, 吾得執而殺之。孰敢?

民眾不怕死, 因何用死來恐嚇他們? 假如民眾常常怕死, 而竟有奇異不正的人出現, 我可以捉拿和殺掉他了。看誰還敢?

199. 常有司殺者殺。夫代司殺者殺, 是謂代大匠斲。夫代大匠斲者, 希有不傷其手矣!

然而, 常道自有掌管殺戮的去殺。你替代掌管殺戮的去殺, 這就叫做替代技藝高超的木匠來伐木了。替代技藝高超的木匠來伐木的人, 很少有不砍傷自己的手呀!

第七十五章 註釋 (635) – (638)

200. 民之饑, 以其上食稅之多。是以饑。

百姓之所以饑餓, 是因為他們的君主享受田地租稅太多。因而饑餓。

201. 民之難治, 以其上之有為, 是以難治。民之輕死, 以其上求生之厚, 是以輕死。

百姓之所以難於治理, 皆因他們的君主要有大作為, 故此難於治理。百姓之所以不怕死, 皆因他們的君主求取財物太多, 故此不怕死。

202. 夫唯無以生為者, 是賢於貴生!

唯獨不貪求財物的君主, 才肯定遠勝那些視財如命、徵收重稅的君主哩!

第七十六章 註釋 (639) – (639)

203. 人之生也柔弱, 其死也堅強。萬物草木之生也柔脆, 其死也枯槁。

人們出生時同樣柔軟, 他們死亡後同樣僵硬。萬物草木長出時同樣柔軟易折, 它們萎謝後同樣乾枯僵硬。

204. 故堅強者死之徒, 柔弱者生之徒。

故此, 僵硬的乃死了的眾物, 柔軟的是活著的眾物。

205. 是以兵強則不勝, 木強則兵。強大處下, 柔弱處上。

所以, 軍隊僵硬就不能取勝, 樹木堅硬就給人砍為木材。堅硬居於下風, 柔軟居於上風。

第七十七章 註釋 (640) – (642)

206. 天之道, 其猶張弓與？高者抑之, 下者舉之。 有餘者損之, 不足者補之。

大自然的規律, 可極似拉弓射箭麼? 弓舉得太高, 就要稍稍把它按低; 按得太低, 便要稍稍把它舉高。亦即有剩餘的, 就要削減它; 不足夠的, 便要補助它。

207. 天之道, 損有餘而補不足。人之道則不然, 損不足以奉有餘。

大自然的規律, 是削減那有剩餘的, 而去補助那不足夠的。人類的規律卻不如此, 是削減那不足夠的, 而去用來送給那有剩餘的。

208. 孰能有餘以奉天下？唯有道者! 是以聖人為而不恃, 功成而不處。其不欲見賢。

誰能夠把有剩餘用來送給天下人呢? 這祇有道呀! 此所以聖人不依仗人去行事, 功業有所成就也不會居功。他更不希望自己有什麼「才能」來炫耀哩。

第七十八章 註釋 (643) – (652)

209. 天下莫柔弱於水, 而攻堅強者莫之能勝。以其無以易之。
天下間沒東西可柔軟得過水, 然而攻擊堅硬卻沒什麼能勝得過它。
因此它是沒東西可以替代的。

210. 弱之勝強, 柔之勝剛, 天下莫不知, 莫能行。
軟的勝過硬, 柔的勝過剛, 天下的人無不明白, 卻不能去實踐。

**211. 是以聖人云:受國之垢, 是謂社稷主; 受國不祥, 是為天下
王。正言若反。**
所以聖人說: 容納國家的恥辱, 這才叫做一國的君主; 容納國家的
不善, 這才叫做天下人之所歸往。合於正道的言論, 乃是容納一切
正反面而同返於道的言論。

第七十九章 註釋 (653) – (662)

**212. 和大怨, 必有餘怨, 安可以為善? 是以聖人執左契, 而不責於
人。**
和解極大的怨恨, 必尚有怨忿餘留, 怎可以會是好事呢? 故此, 聖人
祇拿著用作佐證的田地約契, 而決不會向人們索取田地租稅。

213. 有德司契, 無德司徹。天道無親, 常與善人。
有德的人祇掌管田地約契, 無德的人掌管的是用稅制徹法來徵稅。
大自然之道可沒什麼親或不親的, 祇常常幫助那些喜好道的人。

第八十章 註釋 (663) – (665)

**214. 小國寡民。使有什伯之器而不用; 使民重死而不遠徙。雖有
舟輿, 無所乘之; 雖有甲兵, 無所陳之。**
理想的國家, 是小國少民。理想的治國之道, 是讓十倍百倍之多的
治國工具備而不用; 是讓百姓看重生死而不會移徙遠方。雖有渡船
馬車, 百姓卻不會乘坐它; 雖有軍隊, 國家也不會展示它。

215. 使人復結繩而用之。甘其食, 美其服; 安其居, 樂其俗。

讓百姓恢復舊日用繩子結扣來記事。愛好吃他們簡單的食物, 喜歡穿他們樸素的衣服; 安於住在他們簡陋的居所, 樂於習慣他們樸實的風俗。

216. 鄰國相望, 雞犬之聲相聞。民至老死, 不相往來。

相鄰國家, 接近至可以互相望見; 雞啼聲和犬吠聲, 也可以互相聽見。然而, 它們的百姓, 雖到老死, 亦不會互相來往。

第八十一章 註釋 (666) – (674)

217. 信言不美, 美言不信; 善者不辯, 辯者不善; 知者不博, 博者不知。

真實可信的說話不會漂亮, 漂亮的說話不會真實可信; 喜好道的人不會花言巧語, 花言巧語的人不會喜好道; 明白道的人不會淵博, 淵博的人不會明白道。

218. 聖人不積。既以為人己愈有; 既以與人己愈多。

聖人不會為自己積聚財貨。既然已經把自己的施予他人, 那麼自己就愈為富裕; 既然已經把自己的贈與他人, 那麼自己就愈為豐餘。

219. 天之道, 利而不害; 聖人之道, 為而不爭。

大自然的規律, 乃有利萬物而不會有害; 聖人的規律, 是施與大眾而不會相爭。

註釋 Footnotes

按: 本書註釋乃完整轉錄潘國鍵 (Kwok Kin POON) 與潘君尚 (KS Vincent POON) 合譯《An English Translation and the Correct Interpretation of Laozi's Tao Te Ching 英譯並正解老子道德經》(Toronto: The SenSeis 尚尚齋, 2020) 一書之Footnotes, 以供參考。

Footnotes

(1) "常" here means "immutable and everlasting (恆/久)". See *Kangxi Dictionary* (《康熙字典》).

"常", the "immutable and everlasting", can also refer to Tao (道) and its Manifestation (德) later on in the document. One example can be seen in Chapter 28 Lines 83 and 84.

(2) "天地" is literally "天 (Heaven and skies)" and "地 (Earth)". Together, it refers to the entire Universe.

(3) "德" here is not "virtue" as cherished in Confucianism. For further elaborations, see footnote 4.

(4) Tao (道) can be thought of as the "unidentifiable and nameless (無名)" fundamental way that drives and begets all things in the Universe. Tao also manifests itself to become "identifiable and with names (有名)", the custodian and Mother of all things. Wang Bi (王弼) provided an excellent elaboration on these circumstances:

"凡有皆始於無, 故 '未形'、'無名' 之時, 則為萬物之始, 及其 '有形'、'有名' 之時, 則長之育之, 亭之毒之, 為其母也."
"Everything that exists originated from the unknown void that is indescribable (Tao). Hence, when Tao is 'not yet having any form (未形)' and 'unidentifiable and nameless (無名)', it plays the role of the Originator of all things. Afterwards, when it manifests to 'take form (有形)' and can be 'identifiable and with names (有名)', it rears all, nurses all, perfects all, matures all, and plays the role of Mother of all things."
(interpreted by KS Vincent Poon)
Source: 王弼《老子王弼注》. 台北: 新興書局, 1964, p.003.

Laozi further elaborated on the relationship between "unidentifiable and nameless (無名)" and "identifiable and with names (有名)" in Chapter 40 Line 115:

"天下萬物生於有, 有生於無."

"All things under Heaven sprang from the entity that can be conceived and named, and the entity that can be conceived and named originates from the one that cannot be conceived nor named. "

This "identifiable and with names (有名)", the nurturer and Mother of all things, is referred later on as "Manifestation of Tao (德)" in Chapter 51 Line 139:

"道生之, 德畜之."

"Tao begets all things, the Manifestation of Tao nurtures all things."

Hence, with very few exceptions throughout the document, "德" refers to Tao manifesting itself to become "identifiable and with names (有名)".

The entire *Tao Te Ching* can, therefore, be called *The Book of the Fundamental Way of the Universe and its Manifestation* (道德經).

For further elaborations on "unidentifiable and nameless (無名)", please see Chapter 41 Line 117.

(5) "徼" should be "the fundamental path that all follow (循)", as in *Shuowen Jiezi* (《說文解字》). This is consistent with Wang Bi's (王弼) interpretation of "徼" as "the fundamental path and eventuality of all conceivable things (歸終也)".

"徼", however, cannot be interpreted as "the outer fringe (邊) of Tao". Tao is natural, encompasses all, and homogenous (Chapter 25 Line 74). As such, Tao does not have any inner or outer compartments.

(6) "常無" refers to Line 1's "immutable and everlasting (常道)" and "unidentifiable and nameless (無名)", while "常有" refers to Line 1's" the immutable and everlasting name (常名)" and "iden-

tifiable and with names (有名)".

Line 2 is where Laozi addressed the limitation of his narratives on Tao - if Tao is indescribable, how then can Tao be discussed? Laozi asserted that he could only, at best, use what he called "unidentifiable and nameless (無名)" in the hopes (欲) of examining the indescribable Tao. Similarly, he could, at best, only use what he called "identifiable and with names (有名)" in the hopes of examining the infinitely small and unobservable elements of all identifiable and conceivable entities.

Many, such as Heshang Gong, incorrectly interpreted line 2's "故常無欲以觀其妙" as:

> "人常能無欲，則可以觀道之要."
>
> "Therefore, always possessing no desire shall allow one to examine the essential core of Tao."
>
> (interpreted by KS Vincent Poon)
>
> Source: 《老子河上公注》，卷上, p.1.

Laozi had never asked anyone in *Tao Te Ching* to rid all desire completely:

I. "Desires do arise during their natural propagations (化而欲作)" (Chapter 37 Line 106). Desire is obviously a natural product of Tao and accordingly should not be considered as a hindrance in the study of Tao.

II. "If one plans to diminish an entity, one must first expand it...(將欲歙之, 必固張之...)" (Chapter 36 Line 104). Laozi even discussed how one could apply Tao to achieve certain desirable effects.

III. "Deride selfishness and minimize desires (少私寡欲)" (Chapter 19 Line 59). Laozi had never asked anyone to rid all desires completely, he only asked one to minimize selfish desires.

IV. Wise sages (聖人) have at least this one desire: the desire to follow Tao. Hence, Laozi described them as people who wish to place themselves with Tao "居善地" (Chapter 8 Line 23) and desire no selfish desires "欲不欲" (Chapter 63 Line 175).

Completely ridding all desire may be consistent with some branches of Taoist religion (道教), but that is certainly not consistent with *Tao Te Ching*, the canon of Taoism (道家). This is probably why there are so many incorrect interpretations of "故常無欲以觀其妙; 常有欲以觀其徼" for nearly two thousand years, including that by the renowned Wang Bi (王弼).

The correct interpretation in vernacular Chinese of Line 2 should be:

"故此, 姑且用這個 '常道' 和 '無名', 希望能夠探索一下道的玄奧深妙; 也姑且用這個 '常名' 和 '有名', 希望能夠觀察一下德的萬物規迹."

(interpreted by Kwok Kin Poon)

(7) "玄" was represented as "元" in the *Complete Library in Four Sections* (四庫全書) version of *Tao Te Ching*. "玄" was considered as a taboo character (避諱) in the *Complete Library in Four Sections*, for Qing Emperor Kangxi's given name was "玄燁".

(8) As such, Tao (道), the fundamental way of the Universe, does not discern with the human concept of "beautiful" or "ugly", "good" or "bad".

(9) "Wise sage (聖人)" in Laozi's *Tao Te Ching* is a person who fully comprehends and earnestly follows Tao, which is very different than that of Confucian's.

(10) "Not acting with any personal differentiation and intent (無為)" does not mean one should not act at all. Laozi merely espoused one should act to follow Tao, the fundamental way of the Universe, instead of following one's personal differentiations and intents. Accordingly, one should act to follow the collective mindset of the people (Chapter 49 Line 134) as well as trust what the people trust and distrust what the people distrust (Chapter 49 Line 135).

To interpret "無為" as "one should not act at all" makes no

sense. Laozi certainly acted to author *Tao Te Ching*, and Tao obviously acts to manifest itself to spawn and nurture all in the Universe.

"無為", hence, should not be comprehended to justify "Limited government (小政府)", "Non-interventionism (不干預)", or "Anarchism (無政府)". In fact, recommendations for rulers of states as well as narrations on how wise sages govern were outlined in numerous chapters throughout *Tao Te Ching*. Therefore, Laozi did not reject the idea of a government or go against the enactment of public policies; he merely contended that an ideal government should exclusively follow Tao.

(11) "教" in "不言之教" should be better interpreted as "enlightenment" rather than "teaching/instruction" seen in other interpretations. This is for three reasons:

First, in Chapter 43 Line 23, the same phrase "不言之教" appeared, and it referred to Nature being a source of enlightenment for all. Nature or Tao does not directly teach or instruct us with words. We can, at best, only be enlightened by it.

Second, Laozi abhorred the idea of one being taught acquired knowledge, as indicated in Chapter 20 Line 59 and Chapter 64 Line 175:

"絕學無憂."

"If one insulates oneself from acquiring knowledge and not follow scholarly disciplines, then one shall be free from worries."

"(聖人)學不學."

"(A wise sage) learns not to learn."

Third, in addition to the meaning of "teach", "教" also carries the meaning of "being enlightened (教化)" or "emulate (效)":

I. "教, 效也" in *Guangya - Shigu III* (《廣雅•釋詁三》).

II. "教, 法也" in *Guangyun* (《廣韻•效韻》).

III. "教, 上所施下所效也" in *Shuowen Jiezi* (《說文解字》).

Source: 中央研究院《搜詞尋字》.

(12) "Wordless" here refers to Nature or Tao, for they do not directly teach or instruct us with words. Hence, the subsequent sentence, "All things spring up naturally without diction (萬物作焉而不辭)". See also Chapter 23 Line 69.

(13) Most, if not all, interpret "生而不有, 為而不恃" as "begets all things without claiming ownership, accomplishes all tasks without claiming them as its own achievements". This is incorrect for three reasons:

I. "生而不有, 為而不恃" together can also be found in Chapter 10 Line 30 as well as Chapter 51 Line 140 and, in both cases, is stated as Tao's "Most Mysterious Manifestation (玄德)". How is "begetting all things without claiming ownership, accomplishing all tasks without claiming them as their own achievements" qualify as being the most mysterious and difficult to comprehend?

II. By contrast, our interpretation of this phrase as "begets all without anything and acts without relying on any other" is much more consistent with "Most Mysterious": all things in our known Universe are spawned from something, while implementation of any individual action must be supported by at least one external factor; an entity, therefore, that can beget something out of nothing (無中生有) while acting without any external aid is, indeed, profoundly mysterious.

III. Some, such as renowned scholar Gao Heng (高亨), contended that "恃" carries the meaning of "grace (恩)" and so "為而不恃" should be interpreted as "gives to all things without claiming grace (施澤萬物而不以為恩)" (高亨 《老子正詁》. 上海: 開明書店, 1949, pp. 8-9.). This is highly questionable since Tao simply does not follow the human concept of "grace" (Chapter 5 Line 13: 天地不仁, 以萬物為芻狗). As such, it is inconceivable that Laozi had to spend time to address whether

Tao claims "grace" or not.

"恃" here means "rely on (依)". See *Kangxi Dictionary* (《康熙字典》). The correct interpretation in vernacular Chinese of "生而不有, 為而不恃" should be:

"全無實質而獨自產生, 毫不依仗而獨自作為."

(interpreted by Kwok Kin Poon)

(14) "唯" here is "because", as in:

I.   "冀之既病, 則亦唯君故" in *The Commentary of Zuo - the Second Year of Duke Xi* (《左傳•僖公二年》).

II. "予唯不食嗟來之食以至於斯也" in *The Classic of Rites - Tan Gong II* (《禮記•檀弓下》).

Source: 中央研究院《搜詞尋字》.

(15) "不去" here means "not depart (不離開)", as in *Selections of Refined Literature - Fan Ye - Yi Min Chuan Lun* (《文選•范曄•逸民傳論》): "故蒙恥之賓, 屢黜不去其國." See 《重編國語辭典修訂本》.

(16) "或" here is "invariably/always (常常)" and does not carry its ordinary meaning of "perhaps". According to an annotation of *The Analects - Zi Lu* (《論語•子路》) by Huang Kan (皇侃) , "或" can be interpreted as "常 (always)": "不恒其德, 或承之羞. 皇侃疏: 或, 常也, 言羞辱常承之也." See 中央研究院《搜詞尋字》.

Tao is certainly unlimited and inexhaustible (Chapter 59 Line 161: 莫知其極; Chapter 5 Line 18: 縣縣若存, 用之不勤), and so it is illogical to interpret Laozi had described Tao as "perhaps" inexhaustible.

(17) "似" here is "以", as annotated by Yu Yue (俞樾): "似, 當讀為以, 古以、似通用." See 中央研究院《搜詞尋字》.

This "以", in turn, means "it (其)", as in *Master Lu's Spring and Autumn Annals - Ben Sheng* (《呂氏春秋•本生》) : "非夸以名也, 為其實也." See 中央研究院《搜詞尋字》.

"似" here cannot carry its ordinary meaning of "like" or

"seemingly". Laozi stated that Tao is the fundamental root and origin of all things (Chapter 1). Accordingly, it is unreasonable to interpret Laozi had described Tao here as "only appears to be like" the origin of all things.

(18) "似" here is "it (其)" (see footnote 17), while "或" here is "always (常常)" (see footnote 16).

    "似" here cannot carry its ordinary meaning of "like" or "seemingly", while "或" cannot take its ordinary meaning of "perhaps". Since Tao always exists, it is incorrect to say that Laozi had described Tao as "only seemingly or perhaps" existing.

    The correct interpretation in vernacular Chinese of "湛兮似或存" should be:

        "(道)極其深厚啊! 它是常常存在的!"

        (interpreted by Kwok Kin Poon)

(19) "象" here is "imagine (意想)", as in *Hanfeitzu - Explicating Laozi* (《韓非子•解老篇》): "人希見生象也, 而得死象之骨, 按其圖以想其生也, 故諸人之所以意想者, 皆謂之象也. " See *Kangxi Dictionary* (康熙字典).

(20) "帝" here is "Heaven (天)", as in:

    I. "帝青九萬里, 空洞無一物" in Wang Anshi's (王安石) *Gu Yi* (《古意》). See 中央研究院《搜詞尋字》.

    II. "昔在帝堯, 聰明文思, 光宅天下. 疏: 帝者, 天之一名, 所以名帝" in the *Book of Documents - Yao Dian - Preamble* (《書經•堯典序》). See *Kangxi Dictionary* (《康熙字典》).

(21) The correct interpretation in vernacular Chinese of Line 12 should be:

    "我不知曉這道是誰所生的, 猜想在天出現前便已存在了吧."

    (interpreted by Kwok Kin Poon)

(22) "Straw dogs (芻狗)" were once used in sacrificial ceremo-

nies and were simply discarded when such ceremonies conclud-
ed. See 《重編國語辭典修訂本》.

　　"芻狗" can also be interpreted separately as "straws (芻)"
and "dogs (狗)". In that case, "straws (芻)" represent non-living
objects, while "dogs (狗)" represent living objects. The Universe
treats both types of objects with no mercy.

(23) Such illustrates a key aspect of Laozi's philosophy: the way
of nature is the ideal way for one to deal with all people. Wise
sages merely mirror the Universe's approach in dealing with all
things, which is to treat everything and everyone without mercy
and discernment.

(24) "天地之間" refers to the realm of Heaven and Earth (i.e., the
Universe) and includes all the dynamic interactions within and
between them. "間" is "realm (閒)", as in *The Classic of Rites
- Record of Music* (《禮記•樂記》): "一動一靜者, 天地之閒也."
See *Kangxi Dictionary* (《康熙字典》).

(25) "不屈" here is "endless (不竭/不盡)", as in *Xunzi - Wang Zhi*
(《荀子•王制》): "使國家足用而財物不屈, 虞師之事也." See 《漢
語大詞典》.

(26) "數" here means "arguments (說)", as in:
　　I. "故誦數以貫之, 思索以通之, 為其人以處之, 除其害者以
　　　持養之. 俞樾平議：誦數猶誦說也…凡稱說必一一數之,
　　　故即謂之數. 誦數以貫之, 猶云誦說以貫之" in *Xunzi -
　　　Quan Xue* (《荀子•勸學》).
　　II. "孔子對曰：遽數之不能終其物, 悉數之乃留, 更僕未
　　　可終也" in *The Classic of Rites - Ru Xing* (《禮記•儒
　　　行》).
　　Source: 中央研究院《搜詞尋字》.

(27) "守中" here is "keeping one's original intrinsic idle tranquillity", as annotated by Wang Chunfu (王純甫)："多言數窮, 不如守

中. 中也者, 中也, 虛也, 無也, 不可言且名者也." See 《漢語大詞典》.

"守中" is not "keeping the middle ground". Tao does not follow human points of view, like "good" and "bad", "beautiful" and "ugly" (Chapters 2 and 3). As such, Laozi would have never espoused the idea of taking "the middle ground" between two points of view, for points of view simply do not exist in Tao.

(28) The correct interpretation in vernacular Chinese of Line 15 should be:

"太多說話終會辭窮, 倒不如保持虛靜."

(interpreted by Kwok Kin Poon)

(29) "The Valley Spirit (谷神) " can be regarded as the natural Tao. Some contend it refers to the Spirit of Nurturing, while others see it as the Spirit that is void and mysterious. All interpretations indicate that the Valley Spirit (谷神) is empty and has no shape nor form, and so it can hold, accommodate, and permeate all things.

(30) According to *Kangxi Dictionary* (《康熙字典》), "牝" can be interpreted as "谿谷", which means "the channel at the very bottom between two valleys (兩山間可供流水通過的地帶)", as in *Selections of Refined Literature - Song Yu - Feng Fu* (《文選•宋玉•風賦》): "夫風, 生於地, 起於青蘋之末, 侵淫谿谷, 盛怒於土囊之口." See 《重編國語辭典修訂本》.

(31) "若" here means "is/does/become (乃)", not "seemingly (像)", as in:

    I. "若, 又乃也. 《周語》必有忍也, 若能有濟也." See *Kangxi Dictionary* (《康熙字典》).

    II. "若, 又假借爲乃也." See *Shuowen Jiezi Zhu* (《說文解字注》).

    III. "刑德相養, 逆順若成" in *Mawangdui Silk Texts* (《馬王堆漢墓帛書•十六經•姓爭》). See 中央研究院《搜詞尋字》.

The valve (門) to "The Mysterious Motherly Channel (玄牝)" surely exists, for it is the root of all things (Chapter 5 Line 17), Laozi could not have described it as "seemingly" to exist.

(32) "外" here should be better interpreted as "abandon (棄)", as seen in an annotation by Gao You (高誘): "《呂氏春秋•有度》有所通, 則貪汙之利外矣. 高誘注 : 外, 棄也." See 中央研究院《搜詞尋字》.

(33) See footnote 31.

(34) "幾" here means "nearly resemble (近)". See *Kangxi Dictionary* (《康熙字典》).

(35) "善" should be distinguished from its usual meaning of "good", "nice", or "kind". Tao does not discern and so does not label anything as "good", "nice", nor "kind"; only humans do that (see footnote 8). Accordingly, "善" refers to those who are "well-versed in Tao" or "rich in Tao". See also Chapter 15 Line 46 "古之善為士者".

(36) "淵" here is "abyssal niches (深潭/深池)", as in:
   I. "或躍在淵" in the *Book of Changes - Gan* (《易經•乾》).
   II. "溝流於大水及海者, 命曰川水, 出地而不流者, 命曰淵水" in *Guanzi - Du De* (《管子•度地》).
   Source: 中央研究院《搜詞尋字》.

(37) "與" here means "befriend (親近)", as in:
   I. "公先與百姓而藏其兵" in *Guanzi - Da Kuang* (《管子•大匡》). 郭沫若注 "與, 親也".
   II. "時人憚焉, 莫之或與" in *Baopuzi - Outer Chapters - Content with Poverty* (《抱朴子•外篇•安貧》).
   Source: See 中央研究院《搜詞尋字》.

(38) "仁" here means "individuals (相人偶)". See *Shuowen Jiezi Zhu* (《說文解字注》).

"仁" here does not take on its usual meaning of "benevolence". Since Tao and the wise sages do not follow the concept of being benevolent (Chapter 5 Line 14: 天地不仁, 聖人不仁), Laozi would have never contradicted himself here to describe the distinguished one as being "benevolent".

(39) "正" here is "governance (政)". See *Kangxi Dictionary* (《康熙字典》).

(40) "治" here means "理", which is "ways and principles (道/義理)". See *Kangxi Dictionary* (《康熙字典》).

(41) "事" here means "appoint (任用)", as in *Mo Yze - Exaltation of the Virtuous I* (《墨子•尚賢上》): "是在王公大人, 為政於國家者, 不能以賢事能為政也." See 中央研究院《搜詞尋字》.

(42) The correct interpretation in vernacular Chinese of Line 23 should be:

"身住在喜好道的地方; 心宿在深藏道的靜淵; 結交修養道的
人們; 說話則本於道的誠信; 治理則遵照道的原則; 任用那
依循道的人才; 行動則合乎道的時間."
(interpreted by Kwok Kin Poon)

(43) "已" here is "abandon (棄)". See *Kangxi Dictionary* (《康熙字典》).

Wang Bi (王弼) further elaborated on "持而盈之, 不如其已":

"持, 謂不失德(得)也.既不失其德又盈之, 勢必傾危.故不如
其已者, 謂乃更不如無德無功者也."

"Holding is also known as not losing possession. Not
losing possession and still accumulating shall put oneself
in a more precarious position. As such, 'inferior to those
who abandon' means those who hold and accumulate
are worse off than those who do not hold nor accomplish

anything."

(interpreted by KS Vincent Poon)

Source: 王弼《老子王弼注》. 台北: 新興書局, 1964, p.011.

(44) "揣" here mean "hammer (捶之)". See *Shuowen Jiezi* (《說文解字》).

(45) "梲" should be "銳", which is "to whet" or "to sharpen". See footnote 46.

(46) Wang Bi (王弼) provided an excellent elaboration on "揣而梲之, 不可長保":

"既揣末令尖, 又銳之令利, 勢必摧衄故不可長保也."

"If one hammers the tip of a blade to make it acute and also whets it to make it sharp, then the blade (becomes too weak and) shall eventually break and so cannot be preserved for too long."

(interpreted by KS Vincent Poon)

Source: 王弼《老子王弼注》. 台北: 新興書局, 1964, p.011.

(47) "咎" here is "tragedy (災)". See *Shuowen Jiezi* (《說文解字》).

(48) "遂" here means "accomplished (成)". See *Kangxi Dictionary* (《康熙字典》).

(49) "天" here should be interpreted as "Nature (大自然)", as in the *Book of Changes - The Great Treatise I* (《易經•繫辭上》): "樂天知命, 故不憂." See 中央研究院《搜詞尋字》.

This "天" is different than "天" in "天地", where it means "天 (Heaven and skies)" in footnote 2.

(50) "載" here is "(處)", as elaborated by Wang Bi (王弼): "載, 猶

處也." See 王弼《老子王弼注》. 台北: 新興書局, 1964, p.011.
This "處" is "rest (安)", as in:

I. "昔聖王之處民也, 擇瘠土而處之" in *Discourses of the States - Discourses of Lu II* (《國語•魯語下》).

II. "何以處我? 鄭玄注：處, 猶安也" in *The Classic of Rites - Tan Gong II* (《禮記•檀弓下》).

Source: 中央研究院《搜詞尋字》.

(51) "營魄" here is "魂魄 (soul and mind)". "營" is "竆". "載營魄抱一, 能無離乎. 註: 營, 竆也". See *Kangxi Dictionary* (《康熙字典》). "竆" is "魂". See *Kangxi Dictionary*.

(52) "能無" here is "is it possible to not? (能不?)", as in:

I. "法語之言, 能無從乎？改之為貴" in *The Analects - Zi Han* (《論語•子罕》).

II. "公子侈, 大子卑, 大夫敖, 政多門, 以介於大國, 能無亡乎" in *The Commentary of Zuo - the Thirtieth Year of Duke Xiang* (《左傳•襄公三十年》).

Source:《漢語大字典》.

(53) "專" here is "任", as elaborated by Wang Bi (王弼): "專, 任也." See 王弼《老子王弼注》. 台北: 新興書局, 1964, p.012.
This "任" should be "hold (抱)", as in seen an annotation by Zheng Xuan (鄭玄): "《詩經•大雅•生民》：是任是負, 以歸肇祀. 鄭玄箋：任, 猶抱也." See 中央研究院《搜詞尋字》.

(54) "玄覽" means "the deepest area of the mind that inspects and understands all things (心居玄冥之處而覽知萬物)", as in *Selections of Refined Literature - Lu Ji - Wen Fu* (《文選•陸機•文賦》): "佇中區以玄覽, 頤情志於典墳." See《重編國語辭典修訂本》.

(55) "疵" here is "imperfection (過失/缺點)", as in the *Book of Changes - The Great Treatise I* (《易經•繫辭上》): "悔吝者, 言乎其小疵也. 陸德明釋文：疵, 瑕也." See《漢語大字典》.

(56) "載營魄抱一", "專氣致柔", and "滌除玄覽" are all things that one should not do. To intentionally embrace Tao (載營魄抱一) means one is already absent of Tao in the first place. Trying to become the most gentle is futile, for one can never match the gentleness of a newborn baby, which is the richest in Tao (See Chapter 55 Line 149). Cleansing the mind (滌除玄覽) requires the existence of imperfections in the first place, for one must know what to cleanse. All these actions are futile and ultimately stray away from Tao. One should, therefore, simply "keep one's original intrinsic idle tranquillity" (Chapter 5 Line 15: 不如守中) and allow Tao to naturally act. Accordingly, Line 30 concludes Tao does all, for there is no need for anyone to purposefully do anything to follow Tao. See also footnote 63.

The correct interpretation in vernacular Chinese of Line 28 should be:

"抱持道來安頓自己的魂魄, 能不兩者(道和魂)先已分離嗎？
抱守真氣致使柔軟, 你可及得上嬰兒嗎？ 洗淨心鏡, 能不心
裏先有瑕疵嗎？"

(interpreted by Kwok Kin Poon)

(57) "知" here is "acquired intelligence (智)". See *Kangxi Dictionary* (《康熙字典》).

One should distinguish this "acquired intelligence (智)" from the wisdom of following Tao that Laozi cherished. "Acquired intelligence (智)" refers to a trained or learned wit that is used to manipulate others to serve a purpose. Hence, "acquired intelligence (智)" certainly deviates from the path of Tao. Wang Bi (王弼) nicely elaborated this in his annotations of this phrase:

"術以求成, 運數以求匿者, 智也. 玄覽無疵, 猶絕聖也. 治國
無以智, 猶棄智也. 能無以智乎, 則民不辟而國治之也."
Source: 王弼《老子王弼注》. 台北: 新興書局, 1964,
p.012.

It is also important to recognize that Laozi had never contended a ruler should be ignorant or unintelligent. Laozi merely asserted that rulers should exercise their wisdoms to follow Tao and Nature in their governing; otherwise, they shall face ominous outcomes (Chapter 16 Line 50: 不知常, 妄作凶).

(58) "Valve of Motherly Nature (天門)" refers to the "valve of The Mysterious Motherly Channel (玄牝之門)" seen in Chapter 4 Line 17.

(59) "Motherly/feminine way (雌)" here refers to the puny "motherly" way of the self. One's selfish gentle motherly way contrasts the great gentle feminine and motherly way of the "valve of Motherly Nature (天門)", which is also known as "valve of The Mysterious Motherly Channel (玄牝之門)" in Chapter 4 Line 17. Note "牝" carries the meaning of "feminine/motherly (畜母)". See *Kangxi Dictionary* (《康熙字典》).

(60) "明白" here means "thorough understanding", as in *Zhuangzi - The Way of Heaven* (《莊子•天道》): "夫明白於天地之德者, 此之謂大本大宗, 與天和者也." See 《漢語大詞典》.

(61) "四達" here means "reaching all corners of the Universe (通達四方)", as in *Zhuangzi - Ingrained Ideas* (《莊子•刻意》)： "精神四達并流, 無所不極, 上際於天, 下蟠於地. 成玄英疏: 流, 通也.夫愛養精神者, 故能通達四方." See《漢語大詞典》.

(62) "為" is better interpreted here as "study and learn (學習/研究)", as in *The Analects - Yang Huo* (《論語•陽貨》)： "人而不為《周南》、《召南》, 其猶正牆面而立也與?" See 中央研究院《搜詞尋字》.

　　Instead of "act", interpreting it here as "study and learn" is more consistent with Chapter 20 Line 15's "絕學無憂" and Chapter 64 Line 175's "學不學". Achieving a thorough understanding of Tao without acquiring human knowledge is a key concept espoused in *Tao Te Ching*.

(63) Like footnote 56, "愛民治國", "天門開闔" and "明白四達"

are all things that one should not do. Ruling and protecting the people (愛民治國) requires one to use acquired intelligence. Monitoring Motherly Nature (天門開闔) requires one to apply one's preconceived motherly way to discern. Achieving a thorough understanding that reaches all corners of the Universe (明白四達) requires one to study and learn human knowledge. All these actions are futile and ultimately stray away from Tao. One should, therefore, simply "keep one's original intrinsic idle tranquillity" (Chapter 5 Line 15: 不如守中) and allow Tao to naturally act. Accordingly, Line 30 concludes Tao does all, for there is no need for anyone to purposefully do anything to follow Tao.

The correct interpretation in vernacular Chinese of Line 29 should be:

> "愛護百姓治理國家, 能不自己運用智能嗎? 大自然陰柔產
> 道閥門開開關關, 能不自己視它做你的陰柔產道嗎? 明白
> 道理通達四方, 能不自己先學習知識嗎?"
>
> (interpreted by Kwok Kin Poon)

(64) "畜" here is "nurtures and rears (養育)", as in the *Book of Odes - Odes Of Bei - Ri Yue* (《詩經•邶風•日月》) : "父兮母兮, 畜我不卒. 朱熹注 : 畜, 養." See 中央研究院《搜詞尋字》.

(65) See footnote 13.

(66) Ibid.

(67) "長" here should be better interpreted as "oversee/supervise (主管/執掌)", as seen in the following:
   I.   "故可使治國者使治國, 可使長官者使長官, 可使治邑者
        使治邑" in *Mo Yze - Exaltation of the Virtuous II* (《墨子•尚賢中》).
   II. "使一郡皆寒, 賢者長一縣, 一縣之界能獨溫乎?" in *Lunheng - Ganxu* (《論衡•感虛》).
   III. "許由鞠躬, 辭長九州" in Xi Kang's (嵇康) *Admonitions to the Emperor from the Imperial Mentor* (《太師箴》).

Source: 中央研究院《搜詞尋字》.

(68) See Line 140, as well as footnote 13.

(69) "Hub (轂)" is the hole in the centre of a wooden wheel to which the axle is attached.

(70) "當" here is "at (在)", as in *The Commentary of Zuo - the Ninth Year of Duke Xiang* (《左傳‧襄公九年》) : "當今吾不能與晉爭." See 中央研究院《搜詞尋字》.

(71) If the hole of the hub is completely filled with no empty space, then the axle can never be placed. This then renders the wheel useless.

(72) "埏埴" here means "the process of using water and clay to produce pottery vessels (用水和泥來製作陶器)", as in Kuan Huan's (桓寬) *Yan Tie Lun*《鹽鐵論》: "鑄金為鉏, 埏埴為器." See 《重編國語辭典修訂本》.

(73) "爽" here means "impair (損壞)", as in *Guangya - Shigu IV* (《廣雅‧釋詁四》) : "爽, 傷也." See 中央研究院《搜詞尋字》.

(74) "妨" here means "harm/obstruct (損害/阻礙)", as in *The Commentary of Zuo - the Third Year of Duke Yin* (《左傳‧隱公三年》): "且夫賤妨貴, 少陵長, 遠間親, 新間舊, 小加大, 淫破義, 所謂六逆也." See《重編國語辭典修訂本》.

(75) "腹" here refers to "果腹", which means "only filling the stomach (填飽肚子)", as in Liu Zongyuan's (柳宗元) *Zeng Wang Sun Wen* (《憎王孫文》) : "充嗛果腹兮, 驕傲驩欣." See 《重編國語辭典修訂本》.
　　See also line 8 for the same "腹".

(76) "為腹不為目" is well explained by Wang Bi (王弼):

"為腹者以物養己, 為目者以物役己, 故聖人不為目也."
"Those who seek to satisfy the basic needs of their
bellies make use of things to nourish themselves, while
those who seek to satisfy their eyes make use of things
to enslave themselves. Thus, wise sages never seek to
satisfy their eyes. "
(interpreted by KS Vincent Poon)
Source: 王弼《老子王弼注》. 台北: 新興書局, 1964,
p.014.

(77) See footnote 31.

(78) "貴" here means "high regard (重視)", as in *Zhengzitong* (《
正字通》): "貴, 尚也." See 中央研究院《搜詞尋字》.

(79) Why "Honour ultimately becomes humiliation"? Wang Bi (
王弼) wrote:
"寵必有辱, 榮必有患, 驚辱等, 榮患同也."
"Honour must be accompanied by humiliation, while glory
must be accompanied by tragedy. Hence, anxiety, humiliation, glory, tragedy, etc. are all one and the same."
(interpreted by KS Vincent Poon)
Source: 王弼《老子王弼注》. 台北: 新興書局, 1964,
p.015.

(80) The correct interpretation in vernacular Chinese of Line 39
should be:
"什麼叫做榮寵和羞辱乃都令人惶恐的呢？因為尊尚的榮寵
總必成為卑下的羞辱. 所以, 得了榮寵乃惶恐, 這和失去榮
寵是惶恐一樣."
(interpreted by Kwok Kin Poon)

(81) "愛" here is "cherish (愛惜)", as in:
   I. "是以聖人愛精神貴處靜" in *Hanfeitzu - Explaining
      Laozi* (《韓非子•解老》).

II. "夫鴈順風以愛氣力" in *Huainanzi - Youwu* (《淮南子•
脩務》).
Source: 中央研究院《搜詞尋字》.

(82) "夷" here may take the meaning of "big (大)", as in *The
Book of Odes - Sacrificial odes of Zhou* (《詩經•周頌》): "降福
孔夷." See *Kangxi Dictionary* (《康熙字典》).

(83) "希" here may take the meaning of "tranquil silence (靜寂
無聲)". Heshang Gong (河上公) annotated "希" here as "無聲曰
希", while Lu Deming (陸德明) annotated it as "靜也". See 中央
研究院《搜詞尋字》.

(84) "微" here may take the meaning of "without (無/沒有)", as in:
I. "微管仲, 吾其被髮左衽矣. 何晏集解 : 馬曰 : 微, 無也.
無管仲則君不君、臣不臣, 皆為夷狄" in *The Analects -
Xian Wen* (《論語•憲問》).
II. "微趙君, 幾為丞相所賣" in *Records of the Grand Histo-
rian - Biography of Li Si* (《史記•李斯列傳》).
Source: 中央研究院《搜詞尋字》.

(85) "致詰" here means "thoroughly examined or inquired (究
問)". "致" here means "thoroughly examined (推極/窮究)", as in
The Classic of Rites - The Great Learning (《禮記•大學》): "欲
誠其意者, 先致其知." See 《重編國語辭典修訂本》.
"詰" is "問 (inquired)". "此三者, 不可致詰. 註: 詰, 問也." See
Kangxi Dictionary (《康熙字典》).

(86) The "One" here refers to the "One" found in Chapter 42
Line 119.

(87) "皦" here means "clear and distinct as a gemstone (玉石之
白也)". See *Shuowen Jiezi* (《說文解字》).

(88) "昧" here means "dull (不明)". See *Kangxi Dictionary* (《康

熙字典》).

(89) "繩繩" here means "the appearance of being endless (相續不絕的樣子)", as in *The Book of Odes - Odes Of Zhou And The South - Zhong Si* (《詩經•周南•螽斯》): "螽斯羽薨薨兮, 宜爾子孫繩繩兮." See 《重編國語辭典修訂本》.

(90) "A state of no matter (無物)" here refers to "not yet having any form (未形)" discussed in footnote 2. This "One" in Line 43 ultimately is in "A state of no matter (無物)", which is Tao's form before it begets all things that can be named. This "One" is the intermediate between Tao (道) and its Manifestation (德), as narrated in Chapter 42 Line 119: Tao spawned One; One spawned Two; Two spawned Three; Three spawned all things (道生一, 一生二, 二生三, 三生萬物).

(91) "御" here means "oversee/govern (治理/統治)":
  I. "御, 治也." See *Yupian* (《玉篇•彳部》).
  II. "御, 理也." See *Guangyun* (《廣韻•御韻》).
  Source: 中央研究院 《搜詞尋字》.

(92) "有" here means "territorial realm (州域)", as in:
  I. "方命厥后, 奄有九有. 毛傳：九有, 九州也" in *The Book of Odes - Sacrificial Odes Of Shang - Xuan Niao* (《詩經•商頌•玄鳥》).
  II. "此其所以代夏王而受九有也" in *Xunzi - Jiebi* (《荀子•解蔽》).
  Source: 中央研究院 《搜詞尋字》.

(93) "古始" refers to "the very origin of the ancient past (古代的開始)", as in the *History of the Northern Dynasties - Volume 10 - Northern Zhou Annals - Emperor Gaozu Wu* (《北史•卷十•周本紀•高祖武帝》)："朕運當澆季, 思復古始." See 《重編國語辭典修訂本》.

(94) "道紀" refers to "rules and principles of Tao (道的規律)".
See 《漢語大詞典》.

(95) See footnote 35.

(96) "士" here means "those who are able to deal with their mat-
ters (凡能事其事者俑士)". See *Shuowen Jiezi Zhu* (《說文解字
注》).

(97) "微妙" here means "deeply profound and extraordinary(幽
深而超乎尋常)", as in *Annotations of Mengzi* (《孟子•注疏》) by
Zhao Qi (趙岐): "儒家惟有孟子閎遠微妙, 縕奧難見." See 《重編
國語辭典修訂本》.

(98) "玄通" should be interpreted as "connect with Nature (與天
相通)". "玄" carries the meaning of "nature (天)", while "通" carries the meaning of "arrive to /connect with (達/徹)". See *Kangxi
Dictionary* (《康熙字典》).

(99) "強" here means "barely (勉強)", as in *Strategies of the Warring States - Strategies of Zhao IV* (《戰國策•趙策四》): "老臣
今者殊不欲食, 乃自強步, 日三四里." See 中央研究院《搜詞尋
字》.

(100) "若" here means "is/does (乃)", not its usual meaning of
"seemingly" or "as if". See footnote 31. Laozi had always cherished acting by one's simple primitive nature and would have
never asked one to be pretending or disingenuous.

(101) "容" here means "rules and principles (模式/樣式)", as in
The Rites of Zhou - Office of Winter (《周禮•冬官考工記》) : "
凡為甲, 必先為容. 鄭玄注：服者之形容也, 鄭司農云, 容謂象式."
See 中央研究院《搜詞尋字》.

(102) "將" here is "is/does (乃)", as in *The Book of Expletives* (《

經傳釋詞》): "將, 猶乃也." See中央研究院《搜詞尋字》.

(103) "曠" here means "brilliant and vast (光明/遼闊)", as seen in:

    I. "曠, 明也" in *Shuowen Jiezi* (《說文解字》).

    II. "曠曠, 大也" in *Guangya - Shixun* (《廣雅•釋訓》).

    Source: 中央研究院《搜詞尋字》.

(104) "以" here means "apply/utilize (用/使用)", as indicated in *Yupian* (《玉篇》): "以, 用也." See 中央研究院《搜詞尋字》.

(105) "之" here is often misinterpreted. This "之" actually means "then/consequently (則/就)", as supported below:

    I. "之, 猶則也" in *The Book of Expletives* (《經傳釋詞》).

    II. "鶉之奔奔, 鵲之彊彊. 毛傳：鶉則奔奔, 鵲則彊彊然" in *The Book of Odes - Odes Of Yong - Chun Zhi Ben Ben* (《詩經•鄘風•鶉之奔奔》).

    III. "華則榮矣, 實之不知" in *Discourses of the States - Discourses of Jin VI* (《國語•晉語六》).

    IV. "故民無常處, 見利之聚, 無之去" in *Master Lu's Spring and Autumn Annals - The Second Month of Spring Almanac - Gong Ming* (《呂氏春秋•仲春紀•功名》).

    Source: 中央研究院《搜詞尋字》.

(106) "保" here means "understand (知曉)", as in:

    I. "有勇有義, 非歌孰能保此? 鄭玄注：保, 知也. 孔穎達疏：不是歌聲辨之, 誰能知其有勇有義" in *The Classic of Rites - Yue Ji* (《禮記•樂記》).

    II. "壹心而不豫兮, 羌不可保也. 王逸注：保, 知也. ...顧君心不可保知, 易傾移也" in *Verses of Chu - Nine Pieces - Grieving I Make My Plaint* (《楚辭•九章•惜誦》).

    Source: 中央研究院《搜詞尋字》.

(107) "蔽" here means "hidden/inconspicuous (掩)". See *Kangxi Dictionary* (《康熙字典》). Wang Bi (王弼) further annotated it

as "being covered": "蔽, 覆蓋也." See 王弼《老子王弼注》. 台北: 新興書局, 1964, p.018.

(108) "新" here actually means "親". "親, 又通作新", see *Kangxi Dictionary* (《康熙字典》).

"新" is usually misinterpreted here as "new", which in turn yields two following popular misinterpretations of "夫唯不盈, 故能蔽不新成":

I. "Alas, since they are always not satisfied with themselves (夫唯不盈), they can (故能) break from old traditions (蔽不) and form new ways that are consistent with the times and the way of Tao (新成)."

II. "Alas, since they are content with not being satisfied (夫唯不盈), they are able to preserve their own primitive nature (故能蔽) without establishing any new idea (不新成)."

For I., since Tao is always present with its immutable way, those who follow Tao should recognize there is really nothing new or old in the Universe. Tao is what it is, and so there is no old traditions nor new ways. Accordingly, it makes very little sense to say followers of Tao are pursuing to break something old to form something new.

For II., "蔽" in "能蔽" is obviously a verb, and so cannot be a noun that refers to "primitive nature". Further, it is extremely far-fetched to argue that "able to hide (能蔽)" is a metaphor for "able to preserve primitive nature", for no dictionary has indicated that "蔽" can represent "primitive nature" or the likes.

(109) The correct interpretation in vernacular Chinese of Line 48 should be:

> "誰能夠用靜就令混濁得以漸漸清澈? 誰能夠用長久震動則使安靜得以漸漸產生?(唯有道!) 知曉這道理的人, 不愛自滿. 因為不自滿, 故此才能夠隱藏自己, 決不會說親自成就了些什麼."
>
> (interpreted by Kwok Kin Poon)

(110) "篤" here means "fidelity/diligence (忠誠/專一), as in *Guan-zi - Jun Chen II* (《管子•君臣下》): "小民篤於農, 則財厚而備足." See 中央研究院《搜詞尋字》.

(111) Why must one "nullify oneself to the utmost degree (致虛極)"? All one's accomplishments are actually achieved by Tao, not the self (see Chapter 15 Line 48). Accordingly, one should be humble, tranquil, and disregard the concept of "self" to be able to understand Tao, the fundamental way of all things.

(112) "命" here means "Natural Destiny (天命)", as in *The Analects - Yao Yue* (《論語•堯曰》): "不知命, 無以為君子也. 孔安國注 : 命, 謂窮達之分也." See 中央研究院《搜詞尋字》.

As such, "復命" means "returning to the Natural Destiny". All things spawn from the tranquil and Tao, and so they are destined to return back to this tranquil Tao (Chapter 14 Line 43: 復歸於無物).

(113) Tao spawns and bears all things in the Universe. Therefore, understanding the everlasting and immutable way of Tao empowers one to forebear all things in the Universe.

(114) "王" here should mean "the one who is most desirable (天下歸往)". See *Kangxi Dictionary* (《康熙字典》).

"王" here cannot take its usual meaning of "kings" or "rulers". If so, "王乃天" makes no sense, as not all kings follow the way of Nature.

(115) "天" here should be interpreted as "Nature (大自然)". See footnote 49.

(116) The correct interpretation in vernacular Chinese of Line 51 should be:

"知曉常道, 便會容納一切. 容納一切乃就大公無私; 大公無私乃就萬物所歸往; 萬物所歸往乃就遵循於大自然; 遵循於

大自然乃就依循於道; 依循於道乃就恆久. 這便終身不會危
殆了."
(interpreted by Kwok Kin Poon)

(117) The ideal ruler governs selflessly by way of Tao, and so
the subjects live by their own natures, undisturbed. Hence, the
subjects only know the ruler's existence but not the ruler's governance. Wang Bi (王弼) elaborated on this nicely:

"大人在上, 居無為事, 行不言之教, 萬物作焉而不為始, 故下
知有之而已."

"The ruler, overseeing at the top, governs with no personal differentiation and intent and implements enlightening
others through the wordless. All things merely act but do
not recognize their ruler as the foundation of their lives.
Hence, subjects merely know having a ruler at the top,
nothing more."
(interpreted by KS Vincent Poon)
Source: 王弼《老子王弼注》. 台北: 新興書局, 1964,
p.020.

The correct interpretation in vernacular Chinese of "太上, 下
知有之" should be:

"最好的統治者, 是下面的百姓僅知他的存在(而不知他在統
治)."
(interpreted by Kwok Kin Poon)

(118) For further elaborations by Laozi on this line, please see
chapters 74 and 79.

(119) Tao always acts to deliver consequences that are honest
and impartial (Chapter 21 Line 64: 其精甚真, 其中有信). Accordingly, rulers must be careful in their actions and words, as
illustrated in the subsequence phrase in the same line "悠兮, 其
貴言".

The correct interpretation in vernacular Chinese of "信不足?
焉有不信焉" should be:

"不足信麼？又豈會有不足信的哩!"
(interpreted by Kwok Kin Poon)

(120) "悠" here means "concern (憂)", as in *Shuowen Jiezi* (《說文解字》).

(121) As "言" here refers to speeches by rulers, it should be better interpreted as "decree (號令)", as in *Kangxi Dictionary* (《康熙字典》): "(言)號令也. 《周語》有不祀則修言."

(122) Tao fundamentally does not act according to human moral concepts of "righteousness", "injustice", "benevolence" and "malevolence" (Chapter 5 Line 13: 天地不仁, 以萬物為芻狗). Accordingly, a society that highly regards "benevolence" and "righteousness" shows that its people must have left Tao and are no longer original and simple (樸).

"Benevolence (仁)" and "righteousness (義)" here refers to the Confucian concepts of benevolence and righteousness (仁義). For further elaborations by Laozi on the shortcomings of various Confucian concepts, please see Chapter 38.

(123) Acquired intellect gives rise to human fraud and deception; if a society cherishes too much intellect, then trickery and corruption shall appear. See Chapter 19 Line 57.

(124) The "six kinships (六親)" are one's father, son, elder brother, younger brother, husband, and wife, as annotated by Wang Bu: "六親, 父子兄弟夫婦也." See 王弼《老子王弼注》. 台北: 新興書局, 1964, p.021.

(125) Filial piety is not needed if close relatives are already harmonious among themselves, full of filial piety. Hence, if a society fears losing filial piety, then it is already devoid of filial piety. Laozi often used the argument of "if one fears losing an entity means one is already devoid of that entity" in *Tao Te*

Ching. See Chapter 38 for another notable example.

(126) Loyal subordinates are not needed nor evident when the state is stable and prosperous. Hence, the appearance of loyal subordinates indicates that the state is in chaos.

(127) This "聖" refers to "the sages" instituted by Confucius's thinking, not Laozi's "wise sages (聖人)" who only follow Tao. Hence, "聖" here is translated as "so-call sages".

(128) With no restraint from human-defined morals and knowledge, people can happily live by their own natures.

(129) See Chapter 18 Line 56 and footnote 125.

(130) "令" here means "allow/let (讓)", as in *Strategies of the Warring States - Strategies of Zhao I* (《戰國策•趙策一》): "故貴為列侯者, 不令在相位." See 中央研究院《搜詞尋字》.

(131) "屬" here means "pen (撰寫)", as in:
 I. "懷王使屈原造為憲令, 屈平屬草槁未定" in *Records of the Grand Historian - Biographies of Qu Yuan and Master Jia* (《史記•屈原賈生列傳》).
 II. "以能誦詩書屬文稱於郡中. 顏師古注：屬謂綴輯之也, 言其能為文也" in the *Book of Han - Biography of Jia Yi* (《漢書•賈誼傳》).
 Source: 中央研究院《搜詞尋字》.

(132) "見" means "acknowledge/know(知道)", as in *Huainanzi - Youwu* (《淮南子•脩務》): "今使六子者易事, 而明弗能見者何? 高誘注：見, 猶知也." See 中央研究院《搜詞尋字》.

(133) "素" here means "one's inherent nature (本性)", as in:
 I. "素, 本也" in *Guangya - Shigu III* (《廣雅•釋詁三》).
 II. "是故虛無者道之舍, 平易者道之素. 高誘注：素, 性也"

in *Huainanzi - Chu Zhen* (《淮南子•俶真》).
Source: 中央研究院《搜詞尋字》.

(134) The correct interpretation in vernacular Chinese of Line 58 should be:

"上面這三個觀點由於論述的言辭未算足夠, 故此讓我再有
所撰: 了解本性而持守真樸, 少點自我而捨棄私慾."
(interpreted by Kwok Kin Poon)

(135) The wise never put themselves in precarious situations. See Chapter 50 Line 138: "以其無死地".

(136) "荒" here means "vast (大)". See *Kangxi Dictionary* (《康熙字典》).

(137) "未央" here means "no limit (未盡)", as in *Verses of Chu - Li Sa* (《楚辭•離騷》): "及年歲之未晏兮, 時亦猶其未央." See 《重編國語辭典修訂本》.

(138) "熙熙" here means "the appearance of jolly crowds; all feeling happy, hurried and excited (人來人往, 熱鬧紛紜的樣子)", as in *Records of the Grand Historian - Biographies of Usurers* (《史記•貨殖傳》): "天下熙熙, 皆為利來; 天下壤壤, 皆為利往." See 《重編國語辭典修訂本》.

(139) "太牢" refers to "the process of preparing beef, lamb, and pork for a grand sacrificial ceremony to pay respect to the Universe (古代祭祀天地, 以牛、羊、豬三牲具備為太牢, 以示尊崇之意)", as in *Records of the Grand Historian - Biographies of Jing Ke* (《史記•荊軻傳》): "太子日造門下, 供太牢具." See 《重編國語辭典修訂本》.

(140) "未兆" here means "not yet surfaced (未作之時)", as annotated in *Kangxi Dictionary* (《康熙字典》): "《老子•道德經》我則泊兮其未兆. 註: 意未作之時也."

(141) "孩" here is "smile (小兒笑)". See *Kangxi Dictionary* (《康熙字典》).

(142) "儽" here means "laid-back (懶懈)". See *Kangxi Dictionary* (《康熙字典》).

(143) See footnote 31. Laozi had always cherished acting in one's natural way and would have never asked one to be pretending or disingenuous.

(144) "沌" here means "the appearance of being ignorant and foolish (愚貌)", as in *Kangxi Dictionary* (《康熙字典》): "沌, 愚貌. 《老子‧道德經》忳忳兮.或作沌."

(145) "昭昭" here means "brilliant and conspicuous (明白顯著)", as in Liu Xie's (劉勰) *The Literary Mind and the Carving of Dragons - Zongjing* (《文心雕龍‧宗經》): "故子夏歎書, 昭昭若日月之明, 離離如星辰之行, 言昭灼也." See 《重編國語辭典修訂本》.

(146) "昏昏" here means "obtuse and undiscerning (糊塗不辨是非)", as in *Mengzi - Jin Xin II* (《孟子‧盡心下》): "今以其昏昏, 使人昭昭." See 《重編國語辭典修訂本》.

(147) "察察" here means "discerning (分別辨析)", as in the *New Book of Tang - Biography of Tutu Chengcui* (《新唐書‧吐突承璀傳》): "以黃門直東宮, 為掖廷局博士, 察察有才." See 《重編國語辭典修訂本》.

(148) "悶悶" here means "dim-witted (渾噩)", as indicated in *Ministry of Education Revised Dictionary of Chinese* (《重編國語辭典修訂本》): "悶悶, 渾噩.《老子》第二十章, 俗人察察, 我獨悶悶."

(149) "澹" here means "tranquil (恬静)", as indicated in *Kangxi*

Dictionary (《康熙字典》): "澹, 恬靜也. 《老子•道德經》澹兮其若海." Such interpretation can also be seen in the *Book of Han - Biography of Sima Xiangru* (《漢書•司馬相如傳》): "泊乎無為, 澹乎自持." See 《重編國語辭典修訂本》.

(150) See footnote 31. Laozi had always cherished acting in one's natural way and would have never asked one to be pretending or disingenuous

(151) "飂" here means "the appearance of high winds (高風貌)". See *Kangxi Dictionary* (《康熙字典》).

(152) "以" here means "reason (緣故)", as suggested below :
　　I.　"以, 故也" in *Zhengzitong* (《正字通》).
　　II.　"何其久也, 必有以也" in *The Book of Odes - Odes Of Bei - Mao Qiu* (《詩經•邶風•旄丘》).
　　Source: 中央研究院《搜詞尋字》.

(153) "似" here is "以", which is "and (而)", as annotated by Yu Yue (俞樾): "而我獨頑似鄙. 似, 當讀為以, 古以、似通用...頑以鄙, 猶言頑而鄙也." See 中央研究院《搜詞尋字》.

(154) "食母" here should be interpreted as "the nurturing mother Nature (乳母)". "母" also carries the meaning of "basis/starting point (本)". All are supported by the following:
　　I.　"食母, 生之本也" in Wang Bi's *Laozi's Tao Te Ching with Wang Bi's Commentaries* (《老子王弼注》).
　　II.　"涅非緇也, 青藍也, 茲雖遇其母, 而無能復化已. 高誘注：母, 本也" in *Huainanzi - Chu Zhen* (《淮南子•俶真》). See 中央研究院《搜詞尋字》.
　　III.　"食母, 乳母.《禮記•內則》大夫之子有食母." See *Ministry of Education Revised Dictionary of Chinese* (《重編國語辭典修訂本》).

(155) The correct interpretation in vernacular Chinese of

"眾人皆有以, 而我獨頑似鄙. 我獨異於人, 而貴食母" should be:

"眾人皆有個原因, 而我獨粗鈍兼鄙陋. 我獨不同於人, 而祇崇尚生我育我的大自然."

(interpreted by Kwok Kin Poon)

(156) "容" here means "rules and principles (法則/規律)", as supported by:

I. "容, 法也" in *Guangya - Shigu I* (《廣雅‧釋詁一》).

II. "夫物有常容, 因乘以導之, 因隨物之容" in *Hanfeitzu - Explicating Laozi* (《韓非子‧喻老》).

Source: 中央研究院《搜詞尋字》.

(157) "孔" is "vacuous (空)". Wang Bi (王弼) annotated: "孔, 空也, 惟以空為德, 然後乃能動作從道." See 王弼《老子王弼注》. 台北: 新興書局, 1964, p.024.

(158) "惚恍" here is "in a state of cloudy uncertainty (混沌不清)", as in *Selections of Refined Literature - Pan Yue - Xi Zheng Fu* (《文選‧潘岳‧西征賦》): "古往今來, 邈矣悠哉, 寥廓惚恍, 化一氣而甄三才." See 《重編國語辭典修訂本》.

(159) See Chapter 14 Line 44.

(160) "窈冥" here is "the appearance of unfathomable depth (深遠渺茫貌)", as in *Huainanzi - Lanming* (《淮南子‧覽冥》): "得失之度深微窈冥, 難以知論, 不可以辯說也." See 《重編國語辭典修訂本》.

(161) "精" here is "essence (真氣)", as in:

I. "精, 《增韻》: 真氣也" in *The Essential Comprehensive Dictionary of Ancient and Contemporary Rhymes* (《古今韻會舉要‧庚韻》).

II. "一氣能變曰精. 尹知章注: 謂專一其氣, 能變鬼神來教" in *Guanzi - Xin Shu* (《管子‧心術下》).

III. "吾欲取天地之精, 以佐五穀, 以養民人. 成玄英疏: 欲取窈冥之理, 天地陰陽精氣, 助成五穀, 以養蒼生也" in *Zhuangzi - Letting Be and Exercising Forbearance* (《莊子•在宥》).

Source: 中央研究院《搜詞尋字》.

(162) According to Wang Bi's (王弼) annotation, "信" here means "can be tested (信驗)": "信, 信驗也." See 王弼《老子王弼注》. 台北: 新興書局, 1964, p.025.

(163) See Chapter 1 Line 1, the Name.

(164) See footnote 15.

(165) "以" is "rely on (憑藉/仗恃)", as in:
   I. "富國以農, 距敵恃卒" in *Hanfeitzu - Wu Du* (《韓非子•五蠹》).
   II. "欲知天, 以人事" in *Lunheng - Bu Shi* (《論衡•卜筮》).
   Source: 中央研究院《搜詞尋字》.

(166) "閱" here means "endows (賦與)", as in *Kangxi Dictionary* (《康熙字典》): "閱, 又稟也, 賦與. 《老子•道德經》自古及今, 其名不去, 以閱衆甫. 註: 閱, 稟也. 甫, 始也. 言道稟與萬物始生, 從道受氣."

(167) "衆甫" here is "the birth of all things (物之始也)", as annotated by Wang Bi (王弼). See 王弼《老子王弼注》. 台北: 新興書局, 1964, p.025.

(168) The correct interpretation in vernacular Chinese of Line 64 should be:
   "它(德) 的真氣甚是純正不假, 它裏面有的是可驗證的誠信.
   從古至今, 這德從沒離開過, 靠它來賦與萬物的生長."
   (interpreted by Kwok Kin Poon)

(169) "以此" here means "by the above rationale (此上之所云)", as annotate by Wang Bi (王弼). See 王弼《老子王弼注》. 台北: 新興書局, 1964, p.025.

(170) "曲" here is "submissive and humble (屈曲委細)", as indicated in *Kangxi Dictionary* (《康熙字典》): "《易經•繫辭》曲成萬物而不遺. 疏: 曲, 屈曲委細."

(171) "全" here is "preserve/safeguard (保全)", as supported by:
    I.   "全, 保也" in *Zhengzitong* (《正字通》).
    II. "凡用兵之法, 全國為上, 破國次之" in *The Art of War - Planning an Attack* (《孫子•謀攻》).
    Source: 中央研究院《搜詞尋字》.

(172) It is particularly important to note "曲則全" asks one to be submissive to Tao, not to a ruler. This is supported by a related phrase found in *Zhuangzi - Tian Xia* (《莊子•天下》):
    "人皆求福, 己獨曲全."
    劉文典注: "委順至理則常全, 故無所求福, 福已足矣."
    Liu Wendian's annotation:
    "Those who follow and are submissive to the ultimate
    way of Tao shall always be preserved; hence, there is no
    need for them to seek more blessings, for their blessings
    are already sufficient."
    (interpreted by KS Vincent Poon)
    Source: 劉文典, 《莊子補正》. 雲南: 雲南人民出版社,
    1980, p.999.
Accordingly, Laozi had never asked anyone to submit or bow to a ruler in order to preserve oneself (委曲求全).

(173) "枉" here means "crooked (袤曲)". See *Shuowen Jiezi* (《說文解字》).

(174) The correct interpretation in vernacular Chinese of "曲則全, 枉則直" should be:

"曲從於道就可以保全性命, 彎曲就可以伸直."
(interpreted by Kwok Kin Poon)

(175) "窪" here means "dented/lower levelled (凹陷/低下)", as in the *New Book of Tang - Biography of Nanman II* (《新唐書•南蠻傳下》)："扶南, 在日南之南七千里, 地卑窪." See 中央研究院《搜詞尋字》.

(176) Wang Bi (王弼) elaborated on "少則得, 多則惑" succinctly:

"多則遠其真, 故曰惑也; 少則得其本, 故曰得也."
"The rich are far away from their original and genuine natures; hence, it can be said they can become unsettled. Those who are deficient still attain their original foundations; hence, it can be said they can attain. "
(interpreted by KS Vincent Poon)
Source: 王弼《老子王弼注》. 台北: 新興書局, 1964, p.026.

Indeed, the rich are usually unsettled, for most of them incessantly fear losing their excessive yet unnecessary possessions.

(177) "一" here refers to the singular Tao. See Chapter 10 Line 28 for the same "抱一".

(178) "自見" here means "showing one's brilliance (自我炫耀)", as in Cao Pi's (曹丕) *Discourse on Literature* (《典論論文》)："夫人善於自見, 而文非一體, 鮮能備善, 是以各以所長, 相輕所短." See《重編國語辭典修訂本》.

(179) "伐" here is "accomplishments (功勞)", as seen in:

I. "且旌君伐. 杜預注：伐, 功也" in *The Commentary of Zuo - the Twenty-eighth Year of Duke Zhuang* (《左傳

•莊公二十八年》).

II. "（懷王）非有功伐, 何以得專主約! 顏師古注: 積功
曰伐" in the *Book of Han - Annals of Emperor Gaozu I*
(《漢書•高帝紀上》).
Source: 中央研究院《搜詞尋字》.

(180) See Chapter 41 Line 117.

(181) "飄風" here is "violent winds", as in Cao Pi's (曹丕) *Mis-
cellaneous Poems II* (《雜詩》其二): "惜哉時不遇, 適與飄風會."
See 《重編國語辭典修訂本》.

(182) "從事" here means "follow and serve under (追隨/奉事)"
, as in Niu Sengru's (牛僧孺) *Xuan Guai Lu - Zhang Zuo* (《玄
怪錄•張佐》) : "嚮慕先生高躅, 愿從事左右耳." See 《漢語大詞
典》.

(183) Tao is always honest, impartial, and can continuously
be tried and tested (Chapter 21 Line 64: 其精甚真, 其中有信).
Accordingly, one always faces the eventual and impartial consequences for one's actions without mercy (Chapter 5 Line 13: 天
地不仁, 以萬物為芻狗) as governed by Tao. You reap what you
sow. Such is the gist of Chapter 23 Line 71.
For "信不足? 焉有不信焉", also see Chapter 17 Line 53.

(184) "企" here means "lifting one's heel (舉踵)". See *Shuowen
Jiezi* (《說文解字》).

(185) "跨" here means "踞", which is "crouch (蹲)", as supported
by:
I. "跨, 踞也. 《晉語》不跨其國. 註: 猶踞也." See *Kangxi
Dictionary* (《康熙字典》).
II. "踞, 蹲也." See *Shuowen Jiezi* (《說文解字》).

(186) See footnote 179.

(187) See Chapter 22 Line 67.

(188) "餘食" here means "rotten leftover delicacies", as annotated by Wang Bi (王弼): "餘食, 盛饌之餘也. 本雖美, 更可藏 (藏, 與穢同)也." See 王弼《老子王弼注》. 台北: 新興書局, 1964, p.028.

(189) "行" here is "bodies/shapes (形)", while "贅" here means "ugly tumours (贅瘤)", as annotated by Sima Guang (司馬光): "《老子本義》引司馬光曰：形、行古字通用. 棄餘之食, 適使人厭, 附贅之形, 適使人醜." See 《漢語大詞典》.

(190) See footnote 16.

(191) "物" here can mean "people (人)", as in *The Commentary of Zuo - the Twenty-eighth year of Duke Zhao* (《左傳•昭公二十八年》): "且三代之亡, 共子之廢, 皆是物也......夫有尤物, 足以移人, 苟非德義, 則必有禍." See 中央研究院《搜詞尋字》.

(192) "處" here means "put/situate oneself at (居)". See *Kangxi Dictionary* (《康熙字典》).

(193) The correct interpretation in vernacular Chinese of Line 73 should be:

> "這在道裏面呢, 叫做殘羹穢臭與贅疣醜形. 這都是人們常厭惡的, 故有道的人必不會處身其中."
> (interpreted by Kwok Kin Poon)

(194) "混成" here means "homogenously turbid yet natural (渾然一體, 自然形成)", as in the *Book of Liang - Volume 13 - Biography of Shen Yue* (《梁書•卷一三•列傳•沈約》): "雖混成以無跡, 寔遺訓之可秉." See 《重編國語辭典修訂本》.

(195) On "有物混成, 先天地生", Wang Bi (王弼) further elaborated:

"混然不可得而知, 而萬物由之以成, 故曰混成也. 不知其誰之子, 故先天地生."

"Homogenously turbid and cannot be grasped nor understood, yet, all things spawn from it. Hence, it can be said it is homogenously turbid yet natural. Since one does not know whose offspring it is, therefore, it must have born before the birth of the Universe."

(interpreted by KS Vincent Poon)

Source: 王弼《老子王弼注》. 台北: 新興書局, 1964, p.028.

(196) "寂寥" here means "formless (無形體)", as annotated by Wang Bi (王弼). See 王弼《老子王弼注》. 台北: 新興書局, 1964, p.029.

(197) "殆" here means "tired (疲乏)", as in *Zhuangzi - Nourishing the Lord of Life* (《莊子•養生主》) : "吾生也有涯, 而知也無涯. 以有涯隨無涯, 殆已." See 《重編國語辭典修訂本》.

(198) See Chapter 52 Line 141.

(199) See footnote 99.

(200) "曰" here is an auxiliary particle, as in Yang Shu Ta's (楊樹達) *Ciquan* (《詞詮》): "曰, 語中助詞." See 中央研究院《搜詞尋字》.

An example of such kind of usage can be seen in *The Book of Odes - Odes Of Bin - Dong Shan* (《詩經•豳風•東山》): "我東曰歸, 我心西悲." See 中央研究院《搜詞尋字》.

Hence, in our context, it can be interpreted as "hence".

(201) "逝" here means "flows everywhere in all direction (行也/無所不至)", as annotated by Wang Bi (王弼). See 王弼《老子王弼注》. 台北: 新興書局, 1964, p.029.

(202) "遠" here means "ultimate limit (極)", as seen below:
  I. "遠, 極也. " See 王弼《老子王弼注》. 台北: 新興書局, 1964, p.029.
  II. "極, 遠也" in *Guangya - Shigu I* (《廣雅•釋詁一》)
  See 中央研究院《搜詞尋字》.

(203) See footnote 114.

(204) "域" here is "realm of residence (居處)", as in:
  I. "域民不以封疆之界, 固國不以山谿之險, 威天下不以兵革之利. 朱熹注: 域, 界限也" in *Mengzi - Gong Sun Chou II* (《孟子•公孫丑下》).
  II. "人域是域, 士君子也. 司馬貞索隱: 域, 居也" in *Records of the Grand Historian - Rites* (《史記•禮書》).
  Source: 中央研究院《搜詞尋字》.

(205) "居" here is "takes up (佔/佔據)", as in:
  I. "居, 據也" in *Guangya - Shiyan* (《廣雅•釋言》).
  II. "故為國任地者, 山林居什一, 藪澤居什一, 溪谷流水居什一, 都邑蹊道居什四, 此先王之正律也" in the *Book of Lord Shang - Calculation of Land* (《商君書•算地》).
  Source: 中央研究院《搜詞尋字》.

(206) "法" here means "law (法則)", as annotated by Wang Bi (王弼). See 王弼《老子王弼注》. 台北: 新興書局, 1964, p.030.

(207) The correct interpretation in vernacular Chinese of Line 76 should be:
  "在人居處的地方裏面, 有四個大, 而天下所歸往者佔其中之一. 人取法於地; 地取法於大自然; 大自然取法於道; 道取法於它自己的本然."
  (interpreted by Kwok Kin Poon)

(208) "君" here is "lord (主)", as in *Xunzi - Jiebi* (《荀子•解蔽》): "心者, 形之君也, 而神明之主也." See 中央研究院《搜詞尋字》.

(209) "輜重" here means "supplies that one carries when one travels (外出時攜載的物資)", as in *Records of the Grand Historian - Biography of Su Qin* (《史記·蘇秦列傳》): "蘇秦為從約長, 并相六國. 北報趙王, 乃行過雒陽, 車騎輜重, 諸侯各發使送之甚眾, 疑於王者." See 《漢語大詞典》.

Laozi likened "輜重" to "gravity and prudence (重)" mentioned earlier in the same line, as suggested by Wang Bi's elaboration on "不離輜重":

"以重為本, 故不離."

"(The wise sages) take gravity and prudence as their foundation; hence, they never leave it behind."

(interpreted by KS Vincent Poon)

Source: 王弼《老子王弼注》. 台北: 新興書局, 1964, p.031.

(210) "榮觀" here is "honourable/distinguished (榮名/榮譽)", as seen below:

I. "名者, 脩身慎行, 懼榮觀之不顯, 非所以讓名也" in *Yanshi Jiaxun - Mingshi* (《顏氏家訓·名實》).

II. "臣抱疾東荒, 志絕榮觀, 不悟聖恩, 猥復加寵" in the *Book of Song - Biography of Wang Jinghong* (《宋書·王敬弘傳》).

Source: 《漢語大詞典》.

Heshang Gong (河上公) was incorrect in interpreting "榮觀" here as "宮闕", which means "imperial palace (帝王所居住的宮殿)". Wise sages always wish to preserve their primitive natures (Chapter 15 Line 47: 敦兮其若樸) and be inconspicuous (Chapter 70 Line 191: 被褐懷玉), and so they will never choose to reside themselves in magnificent and flamboyant imperial palaces.

(211) "燕處" here means "at ease (閑居)", as in *The Classic of Rites - Different Teaching of the Different Kings* (《禮記·經解》): "其在朝廷, 則道仁聖禮義之序; 燕處, 則聽雅頌之音." See 《漢語大詞典》.

(212) "超然" here means "transcending above the mundane world (超脫世俗) ", as in the *Book of Han - Biography of Dong Zhongshu* (《漢書•董仲舒傳》): "人受命於天, 固超然異於群生." See 《重編國語辭典修訂本》.

(213) The correct interpretation in vernacular Chinese of Line 77 should be:

> "重是輕的根基, 靜是躁的主宰. 故此聖人外遊時, 笨重的行裝物資整天不會離身(寧願走慢些). 雖然享有榮譽, 抱的也祇會是閑居而超脫世俗的恬靜心態."
> (interpreted by Kwok Kin Poon)

(214) "萬乘" here refers to "a great state (大國)", as in *Strategies of the Warring States - Strategies of Zhao III* (《戰國策•趙策三》): "秦萬乘之國, 梁亦萬乘之國." See 《重編國語辭典修訂本》.

(215) 失君 here means "losing the throne (失君位)", as annotated by Wang Bi (王弼). See 王弼《老子王弼注》. 台北: 新興書局, 1964, p.031.

(216) "轍迹" here means "trace (痕迹)", as in Liang Renfang's (梁任昉) *Da Liu Ju Shi* (《答劉居士》): "行無轍迹, 理絕心機." See 《漢語大詞典》.

(217) "瑕謫" here means "fault (過失)", as indicated in *Ministry of Education Revised Dictionary of Chinese* (《重編國語辭典修訂本》): "瑕謫, 比喻過失. 蘇軾《追餞正輔表兄至博羅賦詩為別》何時曠蕩洗瑕謫, 與君歸駕相追攀. 也作 '瑕讁'."

(218) "籌策" here refers to "an instrument for calculating arithmetic (古時計數之竹筳)", as annotated by Gao Heng (高亨). See高亨 《老子正詁》. 上海: 開明書店, 1949, p.64.

(219) "關楗" refers to "bolts and bars that keep the door shut (關

門的木閂)", as annotated by Fan Yingyuan (范應元): "楗, 拒門木也…橫曰關, 豎曰楗." See 《漢語大詞典》.

(220) "繩約" here means "ties with ropes (用繩綑綁)", as in the *Book of the Later Han - Biographies of Confucian Scholars II* (《後漢書•儒林列傳下》) : "至如張溫 、 皇甫嵩之徒…猶鞠躬香主之下, 狼狽折契之命, 散成兵, 就繩約, 而無悔心. 李賢注：繩約, 猶拘制也." See 《漢語大詞典》.

(221) "救" here means "assist (助)". In *Guangya - Shigu II* (《廣雅•釋詁二》) : "救, 助也." See 中央研究院《搜詞尋字》.

(222) "故" here is "originally in their nature (本來)", as in :
   I.   "故, 本然之詞也" in *The Book of Expletives* (《經傳釋詞》).
   II. "凡禮義者, 是生於聖人之偽, 非故生於人之性也. 楊倞注：故, 猶本也" in *Xunzi - Xing E* (《荀子•性惡》).
   Source: 中央研究院《搜詞尋字》.

(223) "物" here means "affairs/matters (事情)", as in:
   I.   "物, 事也" in *Yupian* (《玉篇•牛部》).
   II. "以鄉三物教萬民而賓興之：一曰六德, 知、仁、聖、義、忠、和; 二曰六行, 孝、友、睦、姻、任、恤; 三曰六藝, 禮、樂、射、御、書、數. 鄭玄注：物, 猶事也" in *The Rites of Zhou - Offices of Earth* (《周禮•地官》).
   III. " (晉威公) 去苛令三十九物, 以告屠黍. 高誘注：物, 事" in *Master Lu's Spring and Autumn Annals - Xian Shi* (《呂氏春秋•先識》).
   Source: 中央研究院《搜詞尋字》.

Wise sages applying Tao to resolve all affairs is an example of Tao's ability to disintegrate all problems and chaos (Chapter 4 Line 11: 解其紛).

"物" should not take the meaning of "all things", for non-living things like rocks do not require any assistance from wise sages.

(224) The correct interpretation in vernacular Chinese of " 是以 聖人常善救人, 故無棄人; 常善救物, 故無棄物" should be:

> "故此聖人常常依循道來幫助人, 本就不會嫌棄任何人; 也常
> 常依循道來幫忙做事, 本就不會厭棄任何事物."
>
> (interpreted by Kwok Kin Poon)

(225) "要妙" here is "profound and wonderful mystery (精深微 妙)", as in Sima Guang's (司馬光) *He Shang Du Yi* (《河上督 役》): "高論探要妙, 佳句裁清新." See 《漢語大詞典》.

(226) "谿" literally means "a ravine at the bottom of a valley where all water naturally migrate toward (水注川曰谿)", as anno-tated in *Kangxi Dictionary* (《康熙字典》): "《爾雅•釋水》水注 川曰谿. 疏: 杜預曰：谿, 亦澗也. 李巡曰：水出於山入於川曰谿. 宋均曰：有水曰谿, 無水曰谷."

Accordingly, in our context, "谿" is the place where all things naturally migrate toward, which means it is the most desirable place for all.

(227) "離" here means "leave (去)", as indicated in *Guangya - Shigu II* (《廣雅•釋詁二》)：" 離, 去也." See 中央研究院《搜詞 尋字》.

(228) Manifestation of Tao encompasses both clear and mud-dy aspects. This is further reinforced in Chapter 41 Line 117: "the cleanest and clearest aspect of the Manifestation of Tao is obscure and muddy (大白若辱)".

(229) "忒" here is "差也 (strayed from)". See *Kangxi Dictionary* (《康熙字典》).

(230) "谷" here is similar to "谿" in Chapter 28 Line 83. The only difference is "谷" is dry without water, while "谿" is moist with water, as indicated in *Kangxi Dictionary* (《康熙字典》): "宋均 曰：有水曰谿, 無水曰谷."

(231) "足" here means "止". See *Kangxi Dictionary* (《康熙字典》). "止" is "reach upon (至)", as in *The Book of Odes - Sacrificial odes of Lu - Pan Shui* (《詩經•魯頌•泮水》) : "魯侯戾止, 言觀其旂. 毛傳 : 止, 至也." See 中央研究院《搜詞尋字》.

(232) Wang Bi (王弼) further elaborated this "樸" as "original and genuine (真也)". See 王弼《老子王弼注》. 台北: 新興書局, 1964, p.034.

(233) "器" here is "all sorts of entities (百行/殊類)", as Wang Bi (王弼) suggested: "真散則百行出, 殊類生, 若器也." See 王弼《老子王弼注》. 台北: 新興書局, 1964, p.034.

(234) "用" here means "administrate (治理)", as in:
  I. "子產相鄭, 病將死, 謂游吉曰 : 我死後, 子必用鄭, 必以嚴蒞人" in *Hanfeitzu - Nei Chu Shuo* (《韓非子•內儲說上》).
  II. "集眾思, 廣忠益, 諸葛孔明所以用蜀也" in *History of Song - Biography of Yu Jie* (《宋史•余玠傳》).
  Source: 中央研究院《搜詞尋字》.

(235) "則" here is "and (而)", as in *The Commentary of Zuo - the Third Year of Duke Zhao* (《左傳•昭公三年》) : "寡人願事君朝夕不倦, 將奉質幣以無失時, 則國家多難, 是以不獲." See 中央研究院《搜詞尋字》.

(236) "大制" here means "administrate via Tao (以大道治理天下)". See 《漢語大詞典》. Also, see footnote 237 for Wang Bi's (王弼) further elaboration on "大制".

(237) "割" here means "to discern (分)". See *Kangxi Dictionary* (《康熙字典》). On "大制不割", Wang Bi (王弼) further elaborated:
  "大制者, 以天下之心為心, 故無割也."
  "Administrating via Tao is to make the mindset of all un-

der Heaven as one's own. As such, one shall not discern
nor discriminate when administrating."
(interpreted by KS Vincent Poon)
Source: 王弼《老子王弼注》. 台北: 新興書局, 1964,
p.034.

(238) "為" here is "rule (治理)", as seen in *Xiao Erya - Expanding
Old Words* (《小爾雅•廣詁》) : "為, 治也." See 中央研究院《搜
詞尋字》.

(239) "已" here is "succeed (成)", as indicated in *Guangya -
Shigu III* (《廣雅•釋詁三》) : "已, 成也." See 中央研究院《搜詞
尋字》.

(240) "神器" refers to "an entity of extraordinary nature" that is
formless, intangible, and cannot be commanded. Wang Bi (王
弼) annotated it as "神, 無形無方也. 器, 合成也. 無形以合, 故
謂之神器也". See 王弼《老子王弼注》. 台北: 新興書局, 1964,
p.034.

(241) "故" here means "after all (畢竟)", as seen in *The Commentary of Zuo - the Ninth Year of Duke Xiang* (《左傳•襄公九
年》) : "利物足以和義, 貞固足以幹事, 然故不可誣也." See 中央
研究院《搜詞尋字》.

(242) "或" here means "is/are/have (有)", as indicated in *Guangya - Shigu I* (《廣雅•釋詁一》) : "或, 有也." See 中央研究院《搜
詞尋字》.

(243) See footnote 191.

(244) "行" here means "the appearance of being emphatic and
assertive (剛健貌)", as in *The Analects* (《論語》): "子路行行如
也." See *Kangxi Dictionary* (《康熙字典》).

(245) "隨" here is "mild and submissive (順應)", as in:

    I.   "隨, 順也" in *Guangya - Shigu I* (《廣雅•釋詁一》).

    II. "禹敷土, 隨山刊木, 奠高山大川" in the *Book of Documents - Yu Gong* (《書經•禹貢》).

    Source: 中央研究院《搜詞尋字》.

(246) "齂" here is "blowing through one's nose (鼻出氣爲齂)", as indicated in *The Exegesis of Six-category Characters* (《六書故》). See *Kangxi Dictionary* (《康熙字典》).

(247) "吹" here is "噓", according to *Shuowen Jiezi* (《說文解字》):"吹, 噓也." This "噓" means "blowing through one's mouth (口出氣爲噓)", as indicated in *The Exegesis of Six-category Characters* (《六書故》). See *Kangxi Dictionary* (《康熙字典》).

(248) "羸" here means "weak and frail (瘦弱)", as in *History of the Southern Dynasties - Biography of Zhou Panlong* (《南史•周盤龍傳》)："形甚羸而臨軍勇果, 諸將莫逮." See《重編國語辭典修訂本》.

(249) "挫" here means "humble (屈折)", as seen in *Zhuangzi - Heaven and Earth* (《莊子•天地》)："不以物挫志之謂完. 成玄英疏：挫, 屈也. 一毀譽, 混榮辱, 不以世物屈節, 其德完全." See 中央研究院《搜詞尋字》.

(250) "隳" here means "wreck or obliterate (毀)", as indicated in *Kangxi Dictionary* (《康熙字典》): "隳與毀通." If one does not "humble (挫)" to Tao, then one shall wreck oneself by Tao. This directly echoes Chapter 22 Line 66: "Ones that are humble and submissive to Tao can be fully preserved (曲則全)."

(251) The correct interpretation in vernacular Chinese of Line 87 should be:

    "畢竟在人裏面, 有些剛健, 有些溫順; 有些慣以鼻呼氣, 有些慣以口呼氣; 有些強壯, 有些羸弱; 有些挫服於道而自全, 有些不服於道而自毀."

(interpreted by Kwok Kin Poon)

(252) "甚" here means "indulgence (溺愛/溺好)", as in *Shuowen Jiezi Zhu* (《說文解字注》) : "(甚)尤安樂也, ...人情所尤安樂者, 必在所溺愛也."

(253) "奢" here means "conceitedness (自誇/誇張)", as indicated in *Selections of Refined Literature - Sima Xiangru - Zi Xu Fu* (《文選•司馬相如•子虛賦》) : "今足下不稱楚王之德厚, 而盛推雲夢以為高, 奢言淫樂而顯侈靡." See 《重編國語辭典修訂本》.

(254) "泰" here means "pride and arrogance (驕縱/傲慢)", as supported by
    I. "泰, 驕也" indicated in *Yupian* (《玉篇》).
    II. "拜下, 禮也; 今拜乎上, 泰也. 何晏集解 : 時臣驕泰, 故於上拜" in *The Analects - Zi Han* (《論語•子罕》).
    III. "是故君子有大道, 必忠信以得之, 驕泰以失之" in *The Classic of Rites - The Great Learning* (《禮記•大學》).
Source: 中央研究院《搜詞尋字》.

(255) The correct interpretation in vernacular Chinese of Line 88 should be:
"故此聖人丟掉溺好, 丟掉自誇, 丟掉驕縱."
(interpreted by Kwok Kin Poon)

(256) "強" here means "violent (暴)", as indicated *Guangyun* (《廣韻•陽韻》) : "強, 暴也." See 中央研究院《搜詞尋字》.

(257) The correct interpretation in vernacular Chinese of "以道佐人主者, 不以兵強天下" should be:
"用道來輔助君主的人, 不會以武力來鎮壓天下."
(interpreted by Kwok Kin Poon)

(258) "好" here means "always easily happen (常常容易發生)", as in Erya (《爾雅•釋草》):"竹篇蓄. 郭璞注：似小藜, 赤莖節, 好生道旁. " See 中央研究院《搜詞尋字》.

(259) "還" here means "counter results (償還/回擊)." See 中央研究院《搜詞尋字》and 《漢語字詞典》.

(260) Why "weeds and thorns (荊棘) shall rise"? The presence of military operations promotes looting and hinders farming. As such, fields will become infertile. Such is succinctly elaborated by Wang Bi (王弼):

> "言師凶害之物也. 無有所濟, 必有所傷, 賊害人民, 殘荒田畝, 故曰荊棘生焉."
>
> Source: 王弼《老子王弼注》. 台北: 新興書局, 1964, pp.035-036.

(261) "壯" here is "mighty and fierce (武力暴興)", as annotated by Wang Bi (王弼):

> "壯, 武力暴興, 喻以兵強於天下者也."
>
> Source: 王弼《老子王弼注》. 台北: 新興書局, 1964, p.036.

(262) "老" here is "frail and wither (衰弱/衰落)", as in:
  I. "老, 朽也" in *Shiming* (《釋名》).
  II. "師直為壯, 曲為老" in *The Commentary of Zuo - the Twenty-eighth Year of Duke Xi* (《左傳•僖公二十八年》.
  III. "治之道, 美不老" in *Xunzi - Cheng Xiang* (《荀子•成相》).
  Source: 中央研究院《搜詞尋字》.

(263) The correct interpretation in vernacular Chinese of Line 91 should be:

> "人若壯猛則必自衰弱, 這叫不依循道. 不依循道, 早就完蛋啦!"

(interpreted by Kwok Kin Poon)

(264) "佳" here means "the finest (善/好)", as indicated in *Shuowen Jiezi Zhu* (《說文解字注》).

(265) See footnote 191.

(266) See footnote 16.

(267) "居" here is "at peaceful times (安)", as in:
   I. "居, 安也" in *Yupian* (《玉篇》).
   II. "豈世世賢哉, 其勢居然也" in *Records of the Grand Historian - Annals of Qin Shi Huang* (《史記•秦始皇本紀》).
   Source: 中央研究院《搜詞尋字》.

(268) For "left" and "right", see Line 94.

(269) "恬淡" here is "simplicity and tranquillity (清靜淡泊)", as in:
   I. "夫虛靜恬淡, 寂寞無為者, 天地之平而道德之至也" in *Zhuangzi - The Way of Heaven* (《莊子•天道》).
   II. "今上治天下, 未能恬佚" in *Records of the Grand Historian - Annals of Qin Shi Huang* (《史記•秦始皇本紀》).
   Source: 《漢語大詞典》.

(270) "樂" here is "desirable (欲)", as indicated in *Jiyun* (《集韻》). See 中央研究院《搜詞尋字》.

(271) "得志" here means "have one's aspirations realized (達到自己的志願)", as in:
   I. "白賁无咎, 上得志也" in the *Book of Changes - Bi* (《易經•賁卦》).
   II. "故四民有業, 各以得志為樂, 惟達者為能通之" in *Selections of Refined Literature - Xi Kang - Yu Shan Ju Yuan Jue Jiao Shu* (《文選•嵇康•與山巨源絕交書》).

Source: 《重編國語辭典修訂本》.

(272) "尚" here is "honour (尊崇/崇尚)", as in:
   I.   "尚, 貴也" in *Jiyun* (《集韻》).
   II. "尚, 崇也, 又尊也" in *Zihui* (《字彙》).
   III. "君子尚消息盈虛, 天行也" in the *Book of Changes - Bo*
        (《易經•剝卦》).
   Source: 中央研究院《搜詞尋字》.

(273) It can be said then that the commanding general-in-chief who oversees more killings carries more bad omen.

(274) "處" here is "treat and deal with (處置/辦理)", as in *Records of the Three Kingdoms - Book of Shu - Biography of Zhuge Liang* (《三國志•蜀志•諸葛亮傳》) : "將軍量力而處之." See 中央研究院《搜詞尋字》.

(275) "悲泣" here is "weep with great sorrows (悲傷哭泣)", as in the *Book of Han - Treatise on Punishment and Law* (《漢書•刑法志》) : "齊太倉令淳于公有罪當刑, 詔獄逮繫長安...其少女緹縈, 自傷悲泣." See 《漢語大詞典》.

(276) "小" here is "puny and humble (低微)", as in *Mengzi - Wan Zhang II* (《孟子•萬章下》): "不辭小官." See 《漢語大詞典》.

(277) "均" here is "potter's wheel (鈞)", as indicated in :
   I.   "漢志曰, 鈞者、均也. 陽施其氣, 陰化其物, 皆得其成就平均也. 按古多叚鈞爲均" in *Shuowen Jiezi Zhu* (《說文解字注》).
   II. "(均)又通作鈞.《書經•泰誓》厥罪惟鈞" in *Kangxi Dictionary* (《康熙字典》).
   This "鈞" here refers to the "Great Potter's Wheel (大鈞) ", which is "Nature (天也)", as further elaborated in *Kangxi Dictionary*:
   "《前漢•賈誼傳》大鈞播物, 塊圠無垠.註: 如淳曰：陶者作

器于鈞上, 此以造物爲大鈞也. 言造化爲人, 亦猶陶之造瓦
耳."

It can be said then that the people can be naturally enlightened and uplifted by Nature (大鈞) from above as if clays naturally rise towards the top as the "potter's wheel (鈞)" spins.
In the *Book of Han - Biography of Dong Zhongshu* (《漢書•董
仲舒傳》), this analogy was used as a metaphor for the people
(the clay below) following their ruler (towards the top):

"夫上之化下, 下之從上, 猶泥之在鈞."

"Alas, the ones above (rulers) enlighten and uplift the
ones below (the people), the ones below follow the ones
above. This is as if clays naturally rise on a potter's
wheel."

(interpreted by KS Vincent Poon)

Source: 《重編國語辭典修訂本》.

As such, "自均" actually means "to naturally follow the ruler".
Most, however, contend "均" is "evenly (平均)" or "equitably (
公平)" and link "民莫之令而自均" with "天地相合, 以降甘露" to
generate the following incorrect interpretation:

"When Nature and Earth work together, the rain naturally
drops from the skies evenly and equitably without any
command from the people."

This interpretation is incorrect because:

I.   The phrase "民莫之令" obviously means "people (民)"
     "need not be commanded (莫之令)", and so "民莫之令"
     has nothing to do with Nature.

II. Tao does not act "evenly" or "equitably", for it does not
     follow the human concept of benevolence (Chapter
     5 Line 13: 天地不仁, 以萬物為芻狗). As such, Tao
     allows natural disasters to occur without relief. Indeed,
     there are plenty of catastrophic floods and droughts
     each year around the world. Why no relief from Tao?
     Even wise sages do not know (Chapter 73 Line 196: 聖
     人猶難之).

III. This chapter focuses on advising rulers. It makes little sense for Laozi here to have stated "Tao acts without any command from the people". Further, by default, people can never command Tao, so Laozi would have been unreasonable and unnecessary to say it here.

(278) The correct interpretation in vernacular Chinese of "民莫之令而自均" should be:

"百姓無需命令, 也自會遵從上面的君主."

(interpreted by Kwok Kin Poon)

(279) See Chapter 1 Line 1.

(280) "制" here is "make/generate (製造)", as in:
    I.   "制, 造也" in *Zihui* (《字彙•刀部》).
    II. "制彼裳衣, 勿士行枚" in *The Book of Odes - Odes Of Bin - Dong Shan* (《詩經•豳風•東山》).
  Source: 中央研究院《搜詞尋字》.

(281) "Identifiable and with names (有名)" here is "Manifestation of Tao (德)". See Chapter 1 Line 1.

(282) See Chapter 1 Line 1.

(283) "知止" here is "to know where to reach and when to stop (知其所應止之處)", as in *The Classic of Rites - The Great Learning* (《禮記•大學》): "知止而后有定, 定而后能靜. 朱熹《章句》, 止者, 所當止之地, 即至善之所在也." See 《重編國語辭典修訂本》.

(284) The correct interpretation in vernacular Chinese of Line 96 should be:

"道生出了德. 德既已有, 便須知道自己所應至和所應停的地方. 知道自己所應至和所應停的地方, 就可以沒危殆了."

(interpreted Kwok Kin Poon)

(285) "譬" here is "understand (通曉)", as in the *Book of the Later Han - Biography of Bao Yong* (《後漢書•鮑永傳》) : "若乃言之者雖誠, 而聞之未譬. 李賢注：譬, 猶曉也." See 中央研究院《搜詞尋字》.

(286) See Chapter 16 Line 50.

(287) This is because overcoming one's selfish desires to follow the natural and selfless Tao is next to impossible.

(288) "強行" is "steadfastly act (勤能行之)", as annotated by Wang Bi (王弼):
> "勤能行之, 其志必獲, 故曰強行者有志矣."
> Source: 王弼《老子王弼注》. 台北: 新興書局, 1964, p.039.

(289) "有志" is "have one's aspirations realized (其志必獲)". Ibid.

(290) "所" here is "the way or principle (道/理)", as in *The Classic of Rites - Questions of Duke Ai* (《禮記•哀公問》) : "求得當欲, 不以其所. 鄭玄注：所, 猶道也." See 中央研究院《搜詞尋字》.

(291) Why "not losing the way of Tao enables one to last long"? Wang Bi (王弼) annotated:
> "以明自察, 量力而行, 不失其所, 必獲久長矣."
> "Applying Tao's enlightenment to introspect oneself makes one act according to one's capacity, and so one shall not lose one's way in following Tao. Hence, one shall be able to last long indeed."
> (interpreted by KS Vincent Poon)
> Source: 王弼《老子王弼注》. 台北: 新興書局, 1964, p.039.

(292) How can one die but not perish? Wang Bi (王弼) annotat-

ed:

"身沒而道猶存."

"The body is gone, yet one's way of Tao still exists."

(interpreted by KS Vincent Poon)

Source: 王弼《老子王弼注》. 台北: 新興書局, 1964, p.040.

One's body always expires and shall eventually return to the eternal Tao (Chapter 16 Line 49: 各復歸其根), but one's way of Tao lives on forever.

(293) "氾" here is "flows and permeates everywhere (氾濫/無所不適)", as annotated by Wang Bi (王弼): "言道氾濫, 無所不適." See 王弼《老子王弼注》. 台北: 新興書局, 1964, p.040.

(294) "左右" here is "applies itself in all directions and so influences all", as annotated by Wang Bi (王弼): "可左右上下周旋而用, 則無所不至也." See 王弼《老子王弼注》. 台北: 新興書局, 1964, p.040.

(295) "衣" here is "encompasses and embraces (覆蓋)", as in *Guanzi - Du Di* (《管子•度地》) : "大雨, 堤防可衣者衣之." See 中央研究院《搜詞尋字》.

(296) "終" here is "always (常)", as in *Mo Yze - Exaltation of the Virtuous I* (《墨子•尚賢上》): "故官無常貴, 而民無終賤." See 中央研究院《搜詞尋字》.

Accordingly, "終不" means "always no" or "never".

(297) "大象" refers to the phenomenon manifested by Tao. This same "大象" can also be seen in Chapter 41 Line 117.

(298) "往" here is "follow and yearn for (歸向)", as indicated in *Jiyun* (《集韻》) : "往, 歸嚮也." See 中央研究院《搜詞尋字》.

(299) "餌" here is "delicacies (餅/饌)", as indicated in *Kangxi*

Dictionary (《康熙字典》).

(300) "過客" here is "passing guests (旅客)" as in Hanfeitzu - Wu Du (《韓非子•五蠹》) : "非疏骨肉愛過客也, 多少之心異也." See 《漢語大詞典》.

(301) "止" here is "an auxiliary word used at the end of a sentence as an intonation (語氣助詞)", as in:
  I. "止, 語末助詞" in *Ciqua* (《詞詮》).
  II. "既曰歸止, 曷又懷止? 高亨注 : 止, 語氣詞" in The Book of Odes - Odes Of Qi - Nan Shan 《詩經•齊風•南山》.
  Source: 中央研究院 《搜詞尋字》.

(302) "出口" here means "expressed in or described with words(出言)", as in Mei Yaochen's (梅堯臣) *Feng He Zi Hua Chi Guo Yu Ru Lai Yin Xi Xuan* (《奉和子華持國玉汝來飲西軒》) : "諸君竟相先, 出口論莫奪." See 《漢語大詞典》.

(303) "無味" here means "ordinary and not distinct (平淡無奇)" as in Han Yu's (韓愈) *Song Qiong Wen* (《送窮文》) : "凡所以使吾面目可憎、語言無味者, 皆子之志也." See 《漢語大詞典》.

(304) "不足" here is "cannot (不能)", as in *Xunzi - Zheng Lun* (《荀子•正論》) : "淺不足以測深, 愚不足以謀知." See 《漢語大詞典》.

(305) "既" here is "exhausted (盡)", as in:
  I. "既, 盡也" in *Guangya - Shigu I* (《廣雅•釋詁一》).
  II. "吾與汝既其文, 未既其實, 而固得道與" in *Zhuangzi -The Normal Course for Rulers and Kings* (《莊子•應帝王》).
  Source: 中央研究院 《搜詞尋字》.

(306) "將欲" here means "plan to (將要/打算)", as seen in Li Ba's

(李白) *Zeng Wanglun* (《贈汪倫》): " 李白乘舟將欲行, 忽聞岸上踏歌聲." See 《漢語大詞典》.

(307) "廢" here is "ruin (傾圮/坍塌)", as indicated in *Shuowen Jiezi* (《說文解字》): "廢, 屋頓也."

(308) "興" is "raise and establish (建立)", as in the *Book of Han -Biographies of Yuan Ang and Chao Cuo* (《漢書•爰盎晁錯傳》) : "臣聞漢興以來, 胡虜數入邊地." See 中央研究院《搜詞尋字》.

(309) "Wei (微)" refers to the entity that cannot be held nor grasped. It is manifested by Tao and is part of "One". See Chapter 14 Line 42.

Line 104 outlines the counteracting property of Tao (Chapter 40 Line 115: 反者道之動), which counters one's selfish actions and desires.

(310) If a fish leaves its natural habitat, it will be more likely to be preyed on or captured. Hence, one should not stray away from the natural and nurturing Tao, for one shall be exposed to unnecessary harm (Chapter 16 Line 50: 不知常, 妄作凶).

(311) "國之利器" here is "instruments that benefit the state", which include laws, law enforcement, as well as the military, as seen below:
  I. "利器, 利國之器也." See 王弼《老子王弼注》. 台北: 新興書局, 1964, p.042.
  II. "賞罰者, 國家之利器也, 所以懲惡勸善, 不以喜加賞, 不以怒增刑" in *Annals of Han - Annals of Emperor Yuan I* (《漢紀•元帝紀上》). See 《重編國語辭典修訂本》.

Such instruments should not be heavily relied upon in governing, for the people benefits the most simply by just following Tao.

(312) The correct interpretation in vernacular Chinese of

"國之利器不可以示人" should be:

> "有利治理國家的工具(例如軍隊、律法等), 切不可以輕易展
> 示百姓."
>
> (interpreted by Kwok Kin Poon)

(313) "將" here is "shall/will/must (必)", as in:

    I. "將, 必然之詞也" in *Jing Zhuan Shi Ci Bu* (《經傳釋詞
       補》).

    II. "難不已, 將自斃" in *The Commentary of Zuo - the First
       Year of Duke Min* (《左傳•閔公元年》).

    Source: 中央研究院《搜詞尋字》.

(314) "自化" here means "naturally live and propagate (自然化
育)", as in *The Classic of Rites - Yue Ji* (《禮記•樂記》): "樂者,
天地之和也, ...和, 故百物皆化. 鄭玄注：化, 猶生也." See 中央研
究院《搜詞尋字》.

(315) See footnote 313.

(316) This "unidentifiable and nameless (無名)" is Tao. See
Chapter 1 Line 1.

(317) "亦" here is "merely just (祇是)", as in:

    I. "亦者, 不過之義" in *Jing Ci Yan Shi* (《經詞衍釋》).

    II. "寡人之從君而西也, 亦晉之妖夢是踐" in *The Commen-
       tary of Zuo - The Fifteenth Year of Duke Xi* (《左傳•僖
       公十五年》).

    III. "王亦不好士也, 何患無士" in *Strategies of the Warring
       States - Strategies of Qi IV* (《戰國策•齊策四》).

    Source: 中央研究院《搜詞尋字》.

(318) "將" here is "adhere to (遵奉/秉承)", as in:

    I. "束帛將命于朝. 鄭玄注: 將, 猶奉也" in the *Book of
       Etiquette and Ceremonial - Rites of Courtesy Calls* (《
       儀禮•聘禮》).

II. "人之所以貴於禽獸者, 智慮; 智慮之所將者, 禮義" in
   Liezi - Yang Zhu (《列子•楊朱》).
   Source: 中央研究院《搜詞尋字》.

(319) See footnote 313.

(320) "定" here is "settle in serenity (安)", as indicated in *Shuow-en Jiezi* (《說文解字》).

(321) This "德" here is Confucian "moral virtue (德行)" not Laozi's "Manifestation of Tao (Te, 德)". This is because:

I.   This entire chapter (Lines 108-111) focuses on criticizing Confucian values like "benevolence (仁)", "righteousness (義)", and "propriety (禮)".

II. Manifestation of Tao (德) does not exist in high (上德) or low (下德) levels . In fact, Manifestation of Tao nurtures all things (Chapter 51 Line 139: 德畜之) and so exists without different levels.

III. If "德" here means "Manifestation of Tao", then the subsequent phrase "失道而後德" in Line 110 makes no sense. "Manifestation of Tao" is a display of Tao's action, and so losing Tao would simultaneously lose its Manifestation as well. How then can Manifestation of Tao (德) independently exist without Tao (道)?

(322) "下德不失德, 是以無德" provides one of the sharpest rebukes of Confucius teaching. Laozi reasoned that it is those who inherently lack "morals" will fear losing "morals". Accordingly, those who espouse not to lose "morals", like Confucius, are actually the ones inherently without "morals".

The correct interpretation in vernacular Chinese of "上德不德, 是以有德; 下德不失德, 是以無德" should be:

"上等德行的人無需德行, 因此亦正顯示他本已具有德行; 下等德行的人不想失去德行, 因此反顯露他本來就是沒甚德行."

(interpreted by Kwok Kin Poon)

(323) "以" here is "reason (因也)", as in *The Book of Odes - Odes Of Bei* (《詩經•邶風》): "何其久也, 必有以也." See *Kangxi Dictionary* (《康熙字典》).

(324) Why is there actually no reason for those with benevolence to act? This is because the Universe does not follow the concept of being benevolent (Chapter 5 Line 13: 天地不仁, 以萬物為芻狗), and so ultimately, all their efforts are in vain. There is then actually no point for them to do anything.

(325) "攘臂" here means "rolling up one's sleeves and bare one's arms (捋起袖子, 伸出胳膊)", as in *Mengzi - Jin Xin II* (《孟子•盡心下》): "馮婦攘臂下車, 眾皆悅之." See 《重編國語辭典修訂本》.

(326) "扔" here means "coercively drag (引也)", as indicated in *Kangxi Dictionary* (《康熙字典》).

(327) See footnote 321.

(328) In *Zhuangzi - The Way of Heaven* (《莊子•天道》), Laozi was recorded to have chastised Confucius, a chief proponent of propriety, in a similar manner: "Ah! Master, you are introducing disorder into the nature of man! (意！夫子亂人之性也！)" See James Legge's *The Sacred Books of China, The Texts of Taoism*.

(329) "前識" here is "the ability to foresee (先見之明)", as annotated by Wang Bi (王弼):
"前識者, 前人而識也."
Source: 王弼《老子王弼注》. 台北: 新興書局, 1964, p.048.

(330) "大丈夫" here is "those who have great aspirations (有志氣而勇敢剛毅的男子)", as in *Mengzi - Teng Wen Gong II* (《孟子•滕文公下》) : 「富貴不能淫, 貧賤不能移, 威武不能屈, 此之謂大丈夫." See《重編國語辭典修訂本》.

(331) See Chapter 42 Line 119 for more elaboration on "One".

(332) "貞" here is "proper order (正)" as in:
I. "貞, 正也" in *Guangya - Shigu I* (《廣雅•釋詁一》).
II. "一人元良, 萬邦以貞" in the *Book of Documents - Tai Jia III* (《書經•太甲下》).
Source：中央研究院《搜詞尋字》.

(333) "恐" is "perhaps (恐怕)", as in:
I. "恐, 疑也" in *Guangyun* (《廣韻•用韻》).
II. "學如不及, 猶恐失之" in *The Analects - Tai Bo* (《論語•泰伯》).
Source：中央研究院《搜詞尋字》.

(334) "發" here is "shake and quake (動)", as annotated in *Kangxi Dictionary* (《康熙字典》): "《老子•道德經》地無以寧, 將恐發. 發, 動也."

(335) "貴高" here means "noble (高貴)", as in the *Book of Song - Biography of Wang Jingwen* (《宋書•王景文傳》) : "貴高有危殆之懼, 卑賤有溝壑之憂." See 《漢語大詞典》.

(336) "蹶" here means "overthrow (顛覆)", as in in *Xunzi - Cheng Xiang* (《荀子•成相》) : "主之孽, 讒人達, 賢能遁逃國乃蹶. 楊倞注：蹶, 顛覆也." See 中央研究院《搜詞尋字》.

(337) "Lowly and primitive (下)" can be considered to be "One", for it is the foundation of all things. See Chapter 39 Line 113.

(338) "不穀" here means "incapable (不善)", with which ancient

rulers humbly designate themselves.　This can be seen in *The Commentary of Zuo - the Fourth Year of Duke Xi* (《左傳•僖公四年》)："齊侯曰：豈不穀是為？先君之好是繼, 與不穀同好, 如何？" See 《重編國語辭典修訂本》.

(339) "致" here means "possess (取得)", as in *The Analects - Zi Zhang* (《論語•子張》)："君子學以致其道." See 中央研究院《搜詞尋字》.

(340) "輿" literally means "a carriage (車)".　See *Kangxi Dictionary* (《康熙字典》).

　　"數輿", hence, refers to the number (數) of horses pulling a carriage (輿).　In the Shang-Zhou era (商周時代), the number of horses pulling one's carriage reflected one's social status.　The greater the number of horses, the higher the social status.　Such custom is recorded in the *Book of Song - Li V - Wan Du Ji* (《宋書•禮五•王度記》): "天子駕六, 諸侯駕五, 卿駕四, 大夫三, 士二, 庶人一." See 沈約, 《宋書》卷十八禮五. 北京: 中華書局, 1974 , p.495.

(341) "琭" here should mean "the appearance of a jade stone (玉貌)", as indicated in *The Comprehensive Dictionary of Ancient and Contemporary Rhymes* (《古今韻會》).　See *Kangxi Dictionary* (《康熙字典》).

　　Accordingly, "琭琭如玉" can be interpreted as "appear as a precious jade".

　　In the past, many interpreted "琭琭" as "rare and precious (稀少珍貴)" by quoting an annotation by Heshang Gong (河上公):

> "琭琭喻少, 落落(珞珞)喻多. 玉少故見貴, 石多故見賤. 言不欲如玉為人所貴, 如石為人所賤, 當處其中也."
> Source: 《漢語大詞典》.

　　Heshang Gong was incorrect, for "the middle ground (其中)" is never the ideal position, but the very bottom is.　See Chapter 66 Line 178: "江海所以能為百谷王者, 以其善下之, 故能為百谷王.'"

See footnote 342 for more elaborations on "琭琭如玉".

(342) "珞" here means "a necklace (瓔珞/頸飾)" as indicated in *Yupian* (《玉篇》). See *Kangxi Dictionary* (《康熙字典》).

　　Accordingly, "珞珞如石" can be interpreted as "appearing as conspicuous gemstones on a necklace".

　　Some incorrectly contended "珞珞如石" means "one should be as strong as stones in holding one's principles". This is incorrect, for this directly contradicts Laozi's assertion of the strong shall come to its end very soon . See Chapter 30 Line 91: "物壯則老, 是謂不道, 不道早已."

　　"不欲琭琭如玉, 珞珞如石" advises one not to pursue being showy and conspicuous, even if one is superior or noble. Hence, "wise sages wear rags as their clothing while bearing jades within them" (Chapter 70 Line 191: 是以聖人被褐懷玉). As such, Wang Bi (王弼) also wrote:

> "玉石琭琭珞珞, 體盡於形, 故不欲也."
> Source: 王弼《老子王弼注》. 台北: 新興書局, 1964, p.051.

(343) The correct interpretation in vernacular Chinese of "故致數輿無輿. 不欲琭琭如玉, 珞珞如石" should be:

> "所以, 那些擁有數馬拉動車子的王侯公卿的高貴, 本就是建築在連車子也沒有的貧困平民的低賤之上. 他們當不想自己耀目如珍貴的寶玉, 顯眼如頸上項鏈的寶石."
> (interpreted by Kwok Kin Poon)

(344) 反 is "返", which is "restore/return back (返回)", as in:
  I. "吾自衛反魯, 然後樂正, 《雅》《頌》各得其所" in *The Analects - Zi Han* (《論語•子罕》).
  II. "悔相道之不察兮, 延佇乎吾將反" in *Verses of Chu - Li Sa* (《楚辭•離騷》).
  III. "寒暑易節, 始一反焉" in *Liezi - Tang Wen* (《列子•湯問》).
  Source: See 中央研究院《搜詞尋字》.

(345) "動" here means "action (行動)", as in:
  I. "動, 作也" in *Erya - Shigu II* (《爾雅‧釋詁下》).
  II. "擬之而後言, 議之而後動" in the *Book of Changes - The Great Treatise I* (《易經‧繫辭上》).
  Source: See 中央研究院《搜詞尋字》.

(346) The correct interpretation in vernacular Chinese of "反者道之動" should be:
  "使一切復返於道, 這就是道的力量和行動."
  (interpreted by Kwok Kin Poon)

(347) "建言" here means "a saying from the past (古語/古諺)", as in Yan Fu's (嚴復) *On Our Salvation* (《救亡決論》)："建言有之：天不變, 地不變, 道亦不變." See《漢語大詞典》.

(348) See footnote 31.

(349) "纇纇" here means "rough and uneven (不平)". See《漢語大字典》.

(350) See Chapter 28 Line 83.

(351) 辱 here is "污濁", as indicated in *Guangya - Shigu III* (《廣雅‧釋詁三》)："辱, 污也." See 中央研究院《搜詞尋字》.

(352) "廣" here is "generous and magnanimous (寬廣)", as in:
  I. "廣，闊也。" in *Zihui* (《字彙》).
  II. "漢之廣矣，不可泳思。" in *The Book of Odes - Odes Of Zhou And The South - * (《詩經‧周南‧漢廣》).
  Source: 中央研究院《搜詞尋字》.

(353) "建" here is "steadfast and sturdy (健)", as annotated by Yu Yue (俞樾) in *Zhuzi Pingyi - Laozi* (《諸子平議‧老子》)："建德若偷. 建, 當讀為健.《釋名‧釋言語》曰：健, 建也. 能有所建為也. 是建、健音同而義亦得通. 健德若偷, 言剛健之德, 反若偷惰

也, 正與上句廣德若不足一律." See《漢語大詞典》.

(354) "偷" here is "weak and frail (薄也)". See *Kangxi Dictionary* (《康熙字典》).

(355) "質" here is "primitive and simple (樸實/樸素)", as in:
   I. "原始要終, 以爲質也" in the *Book of Changes - The Great Treatise* (《易經•繫辭》). See *Kangxi Dictionary* (《康熙字典》)
   II. "質, 樸也" in *Yupian* (《玉篇》). See 中央研究院《搜詞尋字》.
   III. "夫君子取情而去貌, 好質而惡飾" in *Hanfeitzu - Explaining Laozi* (《韓非子•解老》). See 中央研究院《搜詞尋字》.

(356) "真" here is "pure and unadulterated (純正/不虛假)", as in *Zhuangzi - Tian Zifang* (《莊子•田子方》): "其爲人也真." See 《重編國語辭典修訂本》.

(357) "渝" here is "become tainted (變汙)", as indicated in *Shuowen Jiezi* (《說文解字》).

(358) "方" here is "rectangular (矩)", as indicated in *Jiyun* (《集韻》). See 中央研究院《搜詞尋字》. For more elaborations on "大方", please see footnote 359.

(359) "隅" here is "corner (角)", as indicated in *Yupian* (《玉篇》). See *Kangxi Dictionary* (《康熙字典》).
   Why "the most rectangular shape has no corners (大方無隅)"? In calculus, countless infinitely small rectangular edges join up to form a circle, which has no corner.

(360) "器" here means "worldly tangible objects (有形的具體事物)", as in the *Book of Changes - The Great Treatise I* (《易經•繫辭上》): "形而上者謂之道, 形而下者謂之器." See 中央研究院

《搜詞尋字》. Also, see "神器" in Chapter 29 Line 86.

(361) The correct interpretation in vernacular Chinese of "大器晚成" should be:

"最大的具體事物(德), 是需要長時間來漸漸完成的."
(interpreted by Kwok Kin Poon)

(362) See footnote 297.

(363) "隱"is "unimaginably and wonderfully (微妙/不可見)", as in:
    I. "隱, 微也" in *Erya - Shigu* (《爾雅•釋詁》). See 中央研究院 《搜詞尋字》.
    II. "探賾索隱, 鉤深致遠, 以定天下之吉凶" in the *Book of Changes - The Great Treatise I* (《易經•繫辭上》). See 中央研究院 《搜詞尋字》.
    III. "隱, 小則不可見" in *Shuowen Jiezi Zhu* (《說文解字注》). See *Kangxi Dictionary* (《康熙字典》).

(364) See Chapter 1 Line 1.

(365) "唯" here is "without exception/only (衹有/衹是)", as in:
    I. "唯, 獨也" in *Guangya - Shigu III* (《廣雅•釋詁三》).
    II. "惟, 獨. 或作唯" in *The Book of Expletives* (《經傳釋詞》).
    III. "盈天地之間者唯萬物" in the *Book of Changes - Xu Gua* (《易經•序卦》).
    IV. "芳與澤其雜糅兮, 唯昭質其猶未虧" in *Verses of Chu - Li Sa* (《楚辭•離騷》).
Source: 中央研究院 《搜詞尋字》.

(366) "貸" here means "supplying and furnishing (施予/給予)", as in:
    I. "貸, 施也. 謂我施人曰貸也" in *Shuowen Jiezi Zhu* (《說文解字注》).
    II. "貸, 予也" in *Guangya - Shigu III* (《廣雅•釋詁三》).

III. "宋公子鮑禮於國人，宋饑，竭其粟而貸之" in *The Commentary of Zuo - the Sixteenth Year of Duke Wen* (《左傳•文公十六年》).
Source: 中央研究院《搜詞尋字》.

(367) For more elaborations on "One", see Chapter 14 Line 43, footnote 90, Chapter 22 Line 66, and Chapter 39 Line 112.

(368) "Two" can be thought of as a pair of complementary opposing forces, be it negative and positive or male and female. In Chinese, these two opposing forces are usually represented as "Yin (陰)" and "Yang (陽)".

(369) "Three" can be thought of as a third entity that is generated by the interactions between the "Two" opposing forces.

(370) See footnote 11.

(371) "強梁" here is "the brutal and the strong (強勁有力/剛強橫暴)", as in Kuan Huan's (桓寬) Yan Tie Lun《鹽鐵論》："剛者折，柔者卷. 故季由以強梁死，宰我以柔弱殺." See《漢語大詞典》.

(372) "不得其死" here means "do not reap a natural and pleasant death (不得善終)", as in *The Analects - Xian Jin* (《論語•先進》)："若由也，不得其死然. 何晏集解，孔曰：不得以壽終." See《重編國語辭典修訂本》.

(373) "父" here is "甫", See *Kangxi Dictionary* (《康熙字典》).
   This "甫 is " starting point/point of origin (始/起初)", as in:
   I. "甫，始也" in *Yupian* (《玉篇•用部》).
   II. "甫，以男子始冠之偁，引伸為始也" in *Shuowen Jiezi Zhu* (《說文解字注》).
   Source: 中央研究院《搜詞尋字》.

(374) The correct interpretation in vernacular Chinese of Line

121 should be:

> "人們所教化的, 我也用它來教化人. '剛強橫暴的人不得善
> 終', 我必用它作為教化的開始."
> (interpreted by Kwok Kin Poon)

(375) "馳騁" here is "runs/gallops freely (自由遊走)", as in *Huainanzi - Jingshen* (《淮南子•精神》) : "血氣滔蕩而不休, 則精神馳騁於外而不守矣." See 《重編國語辭典修訂本》.

(376) "無有" here is "something without shape nor form (不見形相的東西)", as in *Master Lu's Spring and Autumn Annals - Shen Fen* (《呂氏春秋•審分》) : "清靜以公, 神通乎六合, 德耀乎海外, 意觀乎無窮, 譽流乎無止, 此之定性於大湫, 命之曰無有. 高誘注 : 無有, 無形也. 道無形, 無形言得道也." See《漢語大詞典》.

(377) "無閒 (無間)" here is "infinitely small spaces (無間/沒有空隙/極微小處)" as in *Selections of Refined Literature - Yang Xiong - Jie Chao* (《文選•揚雄•解嘲》) : "大者含元氣, 細者入無間. 李善注 : 無間, 言至微也." See《漢語大詞典》.

(378) See footnote 10.

(379) See footnote 11.

(380) "及" here means "attained (至也)", as indicated in *Guangyun* (《廣韻》). See *Kangxi Dictionary* (《康熙字典》).

(381) "多" here means "important (重)", as indicated in *Shuowen Jiezi* (《說文解字》).

(382) "病" here is "suffering (苦)", as in *The Commentary of Zuo - the Sixteenth Year of Duke Xiang* (《左傳•襄二十四年》): "范宣子為政, 諸侯之幣重, 鄭人病之." See *Kangxi Dictionary* (《康熙字典》).

(383) See footnote 283.

(384) "長久" here means "living long (長壽)", as in:
  I. "敢問治身, 奈何而可以長久" in *Zhuangzi - Letting Be*
   and Exercising Forbearance (《莊子•在宥》).
  II. "臣獨何人, 以堪長久, 常恐先朝露, 填溝壑" in Cao Zhi's
   (曹植) *Qiu zi shi biao* (《求自試表》).
  Source: 《漢語大詞典》.

(385) See footnote 31. Laozi had always cherished acting in one's natural way and would have never asked one to be pretending or disingenuous.

(386) "弊" here means "exhausted (竭/盡)", as in *Guanzi - Chi Mi* (《管子•侈靡》) : "澤不弊而養足. 尹知章注：弊, 竭也." See 中央研究院《搜詞尋字》.

(387) "沖" here is "hollow and empty (空虛)", as in:
  I. "沖, 沖虛" in *Yupian* (《玉篇》).
  II. "原流泉浡, 沖而徐盈. 高誘注：沖, 虛也" in *Huainanzi -*
   Yuan Tao (《淮南子•原道》).
  Source: 中央研究院《搜詞尋字》.

(388) "大成若缺, 其用不弊; 大盈若沖, 其用不窮" describes Tao, while subsequent "大直若屈, 大巧若拙, 大辯若訥" applies to humans.

 Applying Tao's way to discuss human social norms and behaviours is a key feature in Laozi's arguments.

(389) "直" here is "strict and proper (正見)", as indicated in *Shuowen Jiezi Zhu* (《說文解字注》): "(直)正見也. 左傳曰: 正直爲正, 正曲爲直. 其引申之義也. 見之審則必能矯其枉, 故曰正曲爲直."

(390) "屈" here is "submissive and yielding (屈服/屈從)", as in

The Commentary of Zuo - the Twenty-ninth Year of Duke Xiang
(《左傳•襄公二十九年》)：“直而不倨, 曲而不屈.” See 中央研究
院《搜詞尋字》.

It is important to note one should only be “submissive and
yielding” to Tao, not to any person or ruler. “大直若屈” is in fact
related to “曲則全” in Chapter 22 Line 66. For further elaborations, please see footnote 172.

(391) The correct interpretation in vernacular Chinese of
“大直若屈” should be:

    “最大的正直, 乃是屈折(於道).”

    (interpreted by Kwok Kin Poon)

(392) Why “the sharpest and the most brilliant is actually
dim-witted”? This is because the truly brilliant ones only follow
Tao without their acquired intellects or personal wits.

Those who act with their acquired intellects are actually fools
that create chaos in the world. See Chapter 18 Line 55: “慧智
出, 有大偽”, and Chapter 38 Line 111: “前識者, 道之華, 而愚之
始.”

(393) “訥” here means “inarticulate (言語遲鈍)”, as indicated in
Shuowen Jiezi (《說文解字》): “訥, 言難也.” See 中央研究院《
搜詞尋字》.

Nature, which is the most eloquent, enlightens us without
any word. Hence, “the most eloquent is inarticulate”.

(394) The correct interpretation in vernacular Chinese of
“躁勝寒, 靜勝熱” should be:

    “疾動或稍克服寒涼, 惟清靜卻終可克服苦熱.”

    (interpreted by Kwok Kin Poon)

(395) “正” here means “true guiding principle (常例/常法/準則)”,
as in *Guanzi - Bai Guan* (《管子•八觀》)：“江海雖廣, 池澤雖博,
魚鱉雖多, 罔罟必有正.” See 中央研究院《搜詞尋字》.

(396) Why tranquillity is the true guiding principle? Tranquillity preserves the true essences of all things, while rash fierceness offends the fundamental natures of all things. Hence, tranquillity trumps all, as annotated by Wang Bi (王弼):

> "躁罷然後勝寒, 靜無為以勝熱. 以此推之, 則清淨為天下正也. 靜則全物之真, 躁則犯物之性, 故惟清淨乃得如上諸大也."
>
> Source: 王弼《老子王弼注》. 台北: 新興書局, 1964, p.056-057.

(397) "卻" here is "retreat/reclaim (返回)", as in:

I. "金龜換酒處, 卻憶淚沾巾" in Li Ba's (李白) *Dui Jiu Yi He Jian* (《對酒憶賀監》).

II. "百川尚有西流日, 一老曾無卻少時" in Duan Keji's (段克己) *Zhe Gu Tian - Qing Yang Xia Dui Jiu* (《鷓鴣天•青陽峽對酒》).

Source: 中央研究院《搜詞尋字》.

(398) "欲得" here means "selfish greed to possess (貪得)", as in *Hanfeitzu - Explaining Laozi* (《韓非子•解老》) : "聖人衣足以犯寒, 食足以充虛, 則不憂矣. 眾人則不然, 大為諸侯, 小餘千金之資, 其欲得之憂不除也." See 《漢語大詞典》.

(399) "彌" here is "further (程度加深)", as in:

I. "彌, 益也" in *Xiao Erya - Expanding Old Words* (《小爾雅•廣詁》).

II. "其曲彌高, 其和彌寡" in *Selections of Refined Literature - Song Yu - Dui Chu Wang Wen* (《文選•宋玉•對楚王問》).

Source: 中央研究院《搜詞尋字》.

(400) As one travels outside and gains more acquired knowledge, one is more likely to be tainted with artificial social norms and concepts. This drives one to be further away from Tao.

(401) "名" here is "comprehend (明)". See *Kangxi Dictionary* (《康熙字典》).

(402) "益" here means "increasing (增加)", as in:
    I. "益, 加也" in *Guangya - Shigu II* (《廣雅•釋詁二》).
    II. "益, 增也" in *Guangyun* (《廣韻》).
    III. "子木懼, 言諸王, 益其祿爵而復之" in *The Commentary of Zuo - the Twenty-sixth Year of Duke Xiang* (《左傳•襄公二十六年》)
    Source: 中央研究院《搜詞尋字》.

(403) "損" here is "diminish (減少/虧損)", as in:
    I. "損, 減也" in *Shuowen Jiezi* (《說文解字》).
    II. "損, 減少也" in *Yupian* (《玉篇》).
    III. "損下益上, 其道上行" in the *Book of Changes - Sun* (《易經•損》).
    Source: 中央研究院《搜詞尋字》.

(404) Why is that "there is nothing that one cannot do"? By acting without any personal differentiation and intent, one has united with Tao. For Tao, there is nothing that it cannot do (Chapter 37 Line 106: "道常無為而無不為").

(405) "取" here is "rule (治)", as in:
    I. "取, 為也" in *Guangya - Shigu III* (《廣雅•釋詁三》).
    II. "成侯嗣公, 聚斂計數之君也, 未及取民也. 俞樾平議：此取字, 亦當訓治, 取民言治民也" in *Xunzi - Wang Zhi* (《荀子•王制》).
    Source: 中央研究院《搜詞尋字》.

(406) "事" here means "great accomplishments (偉立之功)", as indicated in *Kangxi Dictionary* (《康熙字典》): "《釋名》事, 偉也. 偉立也. 凡所立之功也. "
    "無事" is not "do nothing" or "not do anything". Laozi only asked one to leave behind selfish achievements in order to fol-

low Tao to govern properly. This concept is akin to "無為". See footnote 10.

(407) "不善者, 吾亦善之" cannot be "those who are not benevolent (or kind), I am also benevolent (or kind) to them". This is because wise sages do not follow the concept of being benevolent (Chapter 5 Line 13: 聖人不仁, 以百姓為芻狗).

(408) "德" here is "attain (得)", as in :
  I. "德, 得也" in *Guangya - Shigu III* (《廣雅•釋詁三》).
  II. "是故用財不費, 民德不勞, 其興利多矣" in *Mo Yze - Economy of Expenditures I* (《墨子•節用上》).
  Source: 中央研究院《搜詞尋字》.

 "德" here is not "virtue". Since wise sages treat all people with no mercy as if they are straw-made dogs (Chapter 5 Line 13: 聖人不仁, 以百姓為芻狗), they do not follow the human concept of having "good virtue (善德)".

(409) The correct interpretation in vernacular Chinese of Line 134 should be:
  "聖人沒有既定不變的私心, 祇以百姓的心作為自己的心.
  百姓喜好的, 我也喜好他們所喜好的; 百姓不喜好的, 我也
  喜好他們這個不喜好. 這才得到與百姓完全一樣的喜(與不
  喜)."
  (interpreted by Kwok Kin Poon)

(410) "不信者, 吾亦信之" cannot be "those who are not trustworthy, I also trust them". Trusting someone who is not trustworthy is very much against the nature of Tao, for Tao always delivers what one sows. See Chapter 37 Line 71 and footnote 183. Further, wise sages only make the mindset of the people as their own (聖人無常心, 以百姓心為心), and so they distrust what others distrust. See Chapter 49 Line 134.

(411) See footnote 408.

(412) The correct interpretation in vernacular Chinese of Line 135 should be:

> "百姓信服的, 我也信服他們所信服的; 百姓不信服的, 我也信服他們這個不信服. 這才得到與百姓完全一樣的信(與不信)."
>
> (interpreted by Kwok Kin Poon)

(413) "歙歙" here means "the appearance of no prejudice (無所偏執貌)", as annotated by Wang Bi (王弼):

> "聖人之于天下, 歙歙焉, 心無所主也."
>
> Source: 王弼《老子王弼注》. 台北: 新興書局, 1964, p.060.

(414) "渾" here means "primitive simplistic nature (質樸)", as in Sikong Tu's (司空圖) *Xiong Hun* (《雄渾》): "返虛入渾, 積健為雄." See 中央研究院《搜詞尋字》.

(415) What does "become newborn babies (孩)" mean? Wang Bi (王弼) annotated:

> "皆使和而無欲, 如嬰兒也."
>
> "(The wise sages) make all become harmonious and without any selfish desire, just like newborn babies."
>
> (interpreted by KS Vincent Poon)
>
> Source: 王弼《老子王弼注》. 台北: 新興書局, 1964, p.059.

(416) "十有三" is literally "thirteen", which here actually refers to "the four limbs and nine orifices (四肢九竅)".

"有" here is "and (又)", as in *The Book of Odes - Odes Of Bei - Zhong Feng* (《詩經•邶風•終風》): "終風且曀, 不日有曀. 鄭玄箋: 有, 又也." See 中央研究院《搜詞尋字》.

Hence, "十有三" is "ten (十) and three (三)", which is "thirteen". Such usage is often seen in other classics, for instance, "At thirteen, he learned music (十有三年學樂)", in the *Book of Rites - The Pattern of the Family* (《禮記•內則》). See James

Legge's *The Sacred Books of China, The Texts of Confucianism*.

"Thirteen" then refers to the numerical sum of the four limbs and the nine orifices (四肢九竅) of the human body, as annotated by Hanfeitzu (韓非子) :

"四肢與九竅十有三者."

Source: *Hanfeitzu - Explaining Laozi* (《韓非子•解老》) .

The nine orifices (九竅) are the two nostrils, the two ear canals, the two eyes, the mouth, the urethral opening, and the anus.

Many scholars of the past and present, including Wang Bi (王弼) and Gao Heng (高亨), mistakenly took "十有三" as "three out of ten (十分有三分)". See 王弼《老子王弼注》. 台北: 新興書局, 1964, p.061, and 高亨 《老子正詁》. 上海: 開明書店, 1949, p.106.

(417) "動" here is "often (每每)", as in:

I.   "且兵兇器, 雖克所願, 動亦耗病" in *Records of the Grand Historian - Bells* (《史記•律書》).

II. "車輪動盈箱, 舟載輒連柁" in Wang Anshi's (王安石) *Gan Tang Li* (《甘棠梨》).

Source: 中央研究院《搜詞尋字》.

(418) "之" here is "go into (往)", as in:

I.   "之, 往也" in *Erya - Shigu I* (《爾雅•釋詁上》).

II. "百爾所思, 不如我所之" in *The Book of Odes - Odes Of Yong - Zai Chi* (《詩經•鄘風•載馳》).

III. "滕文公為世子, 將之楚, 過宋而見孟子" in in *Mengzi - Teng Wen Gong I* (《孟子•滕文公上》).

Source: 中央研究院《搜詞尋字》.

(419) "死地" here is "in dire and deadly position (必死之地)", as in *Records of the Grand Historian - Biography of Marquis of Huaiyin* (《史記•淮陰侯傳》): "其勢非置之死地, 使人人自為戰." See 《重編國語辭典修訂本》.

(420) "厚" here is "high regard (看重)", as in *Mo Yze - Exaltation of the Virtuous II* (《墨子•尚賢中》): "厚於貨者, 不能分人以祿." See 中央研究院《搜詞尋字》.

(421) The first "生" here is "possessions (財物/生計)", as in *Discourses of the States - Discourses of Zhou III* (《國語•周語下》): "若積聚既喪, 又鮮其繼, 生何以殖? 韋昭注: 生, 財也." See 中央研究院《搜詞尋字》.

The second "生" here is "life (生命)", as in *Xunzi - Wang Zhi* (《荀子•王制》): "水火有氣而無生, 草木有生而無知." See 中央研究院《搜詞尋字》.

The two interpretations above are further support by the *Book of Documents - Pan Geng II* (《書經•盤庚中》): "往哉生生! 今予將試以汝遷, 永建乃家." See 《重編國語辭典修訂本》.

(422) The correct interpretation in vernacular Chinese of Line 137 should be:

"從出生到死亡期間, 生的人, 有四肢九竅的身軀; 死的人, 也有四肢九竅的身軀; 人在生時, 每每往赴必死絕地來犯險, 亦同樣有著此四肢九竅的身軀. 這是件什麼事情呢? 就是為了這身軀而令人太看重自己的財物和性命啊!"

(interpreted by Kwok Kin Poon)

(423) "攝" here is "maintaining (保養)", as in Yuan Hongdao's (袁宏道) *Qi Gai Gao Yi* (《乞改稿一》): "或者斷緣謝事, 靜攝數月, 庶其有瘳." See 中央研究院《搜詞尋字》.

(424) "被" here is "come into (及/到達)", as indicated in:

I. "被, 及也" in *Yupian* (《玉篇》).

II. "光被四表. 蔡沈《集傳》: 被, 及." in the *Book of Documents - Yao Dian* (《書經•堯典》).

III. "北盡塞表, 東被海涯" in Sima Guang's (司馬光) *Ying Zhao Yan Chao Zheng Que Shi Shi* (《應詔言朝政闕失事》).

Source: 中央研究院《搜詞尋字》.

(425) "容" is "to lay/ to apply (用)", as in :

I. "容, 用也, 合事宜之用" in *Shiming* (《釋名》).

II. "是以人稼之容足, 耨之容耨, 據之容手, 此之謂耕道" in *Master Lu's Spring and Autumn Annals - Shen Shi* (《呂氏春秋•審時》).

Source: 中央研究院《搜詞尋字》.

(426) "育" here means "cultivate (培養)", as in:

I. "育, 養子使作善也" in *Shuowen Jiezi* (《說文解字》).

II. "育, 養也" in *Yupian* (《玉篇》).

III. "君子以果行育德. 王弼注：育德者, 養正之功也" in the *Book of Changes - Meng* (《易經•蒙》).

IV. "尊賢育下, 以彰有德" in *Mengzi - Gao Zi II* (《孟子•告子下》).

Source: 中央研究院《搜詞尋字》.

(427) "亭" here is "cultivate (化育)", as annotated in *Kangxi Dictionary* (《康熙字典》): "《老子•道德經》亭之毒之. 註: 亭謂品其形, 毒謂成其質. 毒, 徒篤反. 今作育."

(428) "毒" here is "develop (育)", as annotated in *Kangxi Dictionary* (《康熙字典》). See footnote 427.

(429) "覆" here is "return (回復)" as in the *Book of Changes - Gan* (《易經•乾》): "終日乾乾, 反復道也." 王弼注作"覆". 阮元校勘記："《釋文》復, 本亦作覆." See 中央研究院《搜詞尋字》.

(430) See footnote 13.

(431) Ibid.

(432) See footnote 67

(433) "宰" here means "that which dominates (主宰者)", as in:

I. "宰, 凡為事物之主者亦曰宰" in *Zhengzitong* (《正字

124

通》).

II. "若有真宰, 而特不得其眹" in *Zhuangzi - The Adjust-
ment of Controversies* (《莊子•齊物論》).

See 中央研究院《搜詞尋字》.

(434) See Chapter Line 1 and Chapter 25 Line 74.

(435) "兌" here refers to "the senses of the ears, eyes, noses,
and mouths (耳目鼻口)", as annotated by Gao You (高誘) in
Huainanzi - Tao Ying (《淮南子•道應》) : "王若欲久持之, 則塞民
於兌. 高誘注 : 兌, 耳目鼻口也. 《老子》曰 : 塞其兌也." See 中
央研究院《搜詞尋字》.

(436) "勤" here means "exhausted (盡)", as in *Huainanzi - Zhu
Shu Xun* (《淮南子•主術訓》) : "力勤財匱. 任繼愈注 : 勤, 即
盡." See 《漢語大字典》.

(437) "濟" here means "to achieve (成就)" as in:
I. "濟, 成也" in *Erya - Shiyan* (《爾雅•釋言》).
II. "必有忍, 其乃有濟; 有容, 德乃大" in the *Book of Docu-
ments - Jun Chen* (《書經•君陳》).
Source: 中央研究院《搜詞尋字》.

(438) See footnote 221.

(439) This "Small (小)" is Tao, for Tao is so small that it can
even penetrate infinitely small space (無有入無閒). See Chapter
43 Line 122.

(440) Tao is the gentlest yet oversees the toughest (天下之至
柔, 馳騁天下之至堅). See Chapter 43 Line 22. Therefore, the
gentlest is the source of true strength.

(441) "遺" here "retain (留)", as in:
I. "寧王遺我大寶龜" in the *Book of Documents - Da Gao*

(《書經•大誥》).

    II. "古之遺愛也" in *The Commentary of Zuo - the Nine-teenth year of Duke Zhao* (《左傳•昭十九年》).

    Source: *Kangxi Dictionary* (《康熙字典》).

(442) "殃" here is "harm (災禍)", as indicated in *Guangya - Shiyan* (《廣雅•釋言》): "殃, 禍也." See 中央研究院《搜詞尋字》.

(443) "習" here is "comprehend (瞭解/熟悉)", as in:

    I. "是皆習民數者也" in *Discourses of the States - Discourses of Zhou I* (《國語•周語上》).

    II. "嘗無師傅所教學, 不習於誦. 高誘注：習, 曉" in *Strategies of the Warring States - Strategies of Qin V* (《戰國策•秦策五》).

    Source: 中央研究院《搜詞尋字》.

For further elaborations on this "Immutable (常)", see Chapter 16 Lines 50 and 51.

(444) "介然" here means "unwaveringly (堅定不動搖)", as in *Xunzi - Xiushen* (《荀子•修身》): "善在身, 介然必以自好也." See 《漢語大詞典》.

(445) "徑" here is "narrow paths (小路)", as indicated in *Yupian* (《玉篇》): "徑, 小路也." See *Kangxi Dictionary* (《康熙字典》).

(446) "除" here is "construct (修治)", as in the *Book of Han - Biography of Dongfang Shuo* (《漢書•東方朔傳》): "舉籍阿城以南, 盩厔以東, 宜春以西, 提封頃畝, 及其賈直, 欲除以為上林苑, 屬之南山." See 《重編國語辭典修訂本》.

(447) "朝" here is "mansions (宮室)", as annotated by Wang Bi (王弼): "朝, 宮室也." See 王弼《老子王弼注》. 台北: 新興書局, 1964, p.064.

The correct interpretation in vernacular Chinese of "朝甚除" should be:

"宮室建造太多."
(interpreted by Kwok Kin Poon)

(448) "文綵" is "elegant and colourful dresses (華美的衣服)", as indicated in *Records of the Grand Historian - Biographies of Usurers* (《史記‧貨殖列傳》) : "齊帶山河, 膏壤千里, 宜桑麻, 人民多文綵布帛魚鹽." See 《漢語大詞典》.

(449) "厭" here is "indulge with food (飽/飫)", as in:
  I. "厭, 足也" in *Jiyun* (《集韻》).
  II. "萬年厭于乃德. 陸德明釋文, 馬云 : 厭, 飫也" in the *Book of Documents - Luo Gao* (《書經‧洛誥》).
  III. "原憲不厭糟糠, 匿於窮巷. 司馬貞索隱 : 饜, 飽也" in *Records of the Grand Historian - Biographies of Usurers* (《史記‧貨殖列傳》).
  Source: 中央研究院《搜詞尋字》.

(450) "財貨" here means "wealth and possessions (財物)", as in *Records of the Grand Historian - Annals of Xiang Yu* (《史記‧項羽本紀》) : " 沛公居山東時, 貪於財貨, 好美姬." See 《漢語大詞典》.

(451) "盜夸" here is "great robbers (盜魁)", as indicated in *Hanyu Da Cidian* (《漢語大詞典》). "夸" here is "great (大)", as seen in *Kangxi Dictionary* (《康熙字典》).

(452) "建" here means "institute (樹立)", as in Liu Zongyua's (柳宗元) *Treatise on Feudalism* (《封建論》): "予以為周之喪久矣, 徒建空名於公侯之上耳." See《重編國語辭典修訂本》.

(453) "以" here is "thus (因)", as indicated in *Kangxi Dictionary* (《康熙字典》).

(454) "於" here is "for (為了)", as in *Records of the Grand Historian - House of Duke Tai of Qi* (《史記‧齊太公世家》) : "齊使管

仲平戎於周." See 中央研究院《搜詞尋字》.

(455) "德" here is not Confucius's "moral virtues (德行)". Instead, it is the resulting outcome (i.e., manifestation) of following Tao. Laozi abhorred Confucius's "moral values". See Chapter 38 Line 108 and footnote 322.

(456) "Pure and genuine (真)" here refers to "original simplicity (樸)" as in Chapter 24 Line 84 "常德乃足, 復歸於樸". This is because cultivating Tao for oneself results in one returning to the pure and original simplicity (樸). See also footnote 356.

(457) The correct interpretation in vernacular Chinese of Line 147 should be:
> "為了自身而修養道, 他的德乃就真樸; 為了家庭而修養道,
> 他的德乃就豐足; 為了家鄉而修養道, 他的德乃就更為增長;
> 為了國家而修養道, 他的德乃就更為豐厚; 為了天下而修養
> 道, 他的德乃就更為全面而普及."
> (interpreted by Kwok Kin Poon)

(458) "觀" here is "examine others with one's understanding (以我所了解的來觀察事物)", as in *Shuowen Jiezi Zhu* (《說文解字注》): "凡以我諦視物曰觀." Here "one's understanding" refers to "one's understanding of Tao".

(459) The "above rationale" refers to Chapter 54 Line 147.

(460) "含德" here is "harbouring the Manifestation of Tao (懷藏道德)", as in Xiao Tong's (蕭統) *Preface to The Collected Works of Tao Yuanming* (《陶淵明集序》): "含德之至, 莫踰於道; 親己之切, 無重於身." See 《漢語大詞典》.

(461) "比" here is "the same as (同/齊同)", as in:
> I. "比, 齊也" in *Zihui* (《字彙》).
> II. "比物四驪, 閑之維則. 陸德明釋文：比, 齊同也" in *The*

Book of Odes - Minor Odes of the Kingdom - Liu Yue (《詩經•小雅•六月》).
Source: 中央研究院《搜詞尋字》.

(462) "赤子" here is "newborn babies (初生的嬰兒)", as in the *Book of Documents - Kang Gao* (《書經•康誥》) : "若保赤子, 惟民其康乂. 孔穎達疏: 子生赤色, 故言赤子." See《漢語大詞典》.

(463) Those who richly harbour the Manifestation of Tao only live by their natures and pay no attention to concepts and values set by humans. Accordingly, they are the same as newborn babies.

(464) "據" here means "seize (抓)", as in *Records of the Grand Historian - Annals of Empress Dowager Lu* (《史記•呂太后本紀》) : "呂后祓, 還過軹道, 見物如蒼犬, 據高后掖, 忽弗復見." See 中央研究院《搜詞尋字》.

(465) "攫鳥" here is "fierce birds of prey (鷙鳥/兇猛的鳥)", as annotated by Cheng Xuanying (成玄英): "攫鳥, 鷹鸇類也." See《漢語大詞典》.

(466) Why do fierce animals not attack newborn babies? This is because newborn babies only live by Tao and do not offend anything in nature, as annotate by Wang Bi (王弼):
"赤子無求無欲, 不犯眾物, 故毒蟲之物無犯之人也. 含德之厚者, 不犯於物, 故無物以損其全也."
Source: 王弼《老子王弼注》. 台北: 新興書局, 1964, p.066.

(467) "全" here is "perfectly (完整/完好)", as in:
I. "全, 完也" in *Shuowen Jiezi* (《說文解字》).
II. "得此六材之全, 然後可以為良. 鄭玄注 : 全, 無瑕病" in *The Rites of Zhou - Record of Trades* (《周禮•考工記》).

III. "純粹全犧, 獻之公門. 李善注引孔安國曰：體完曰全"
in *Selections of Refined Literature - Mei Sheng - Qi Fa*
(《文選•枚乘•七發》).

IV. "耄期身未病, 貧困氣猶全" in Lu You's (陸游) *Zi Yi* (《
自貽》).

Source: 中央研究院《搜詞尋字》.

(468) "作" here means "grows and develops (長)", as annotated
by Wang Bi (王弼):

"作, 長也. 無物以損其身, 故能全長也."
Source: 王弼《老子王弼注》. 台北: 新興書局, 1964,
p.067.

(469) See footnote 161.

(470) The correct interpretation in vernacular Chinese of
"未知牝牡之合而全作, 精之至也" should be:

" (嬰兒)不曉得陰氣陽氣相調合, 卻能完好無損地成長, 這可
說是真氣的極致了."

(interpreted by Kwok Kin Poon)

(471) "嗄" here is "a voice that has become hoarse (聲音嘶啞)",
as indicated in *Yupian* (《玉篇》)："嗄, 聲破." See 中央研究院《
搜詞尋字》.

(472) For further elaborations on this "Immutable (常)", see
Chapter 16 Lines 50 and 51.

(473) "益" here means "increase/prolong (增加)", as in:

I. "益, 加也" in" *Guangya - Shigu II* (《廣雅•釋詁二》).

II. "益, 增也" in *Guangyun* (《廣韻•昔韻》).

III. "子木懼, 言諸王, 益其祿爵而復之" in *The Commentary
of Zuo - the Twenty-sixth Year of Duke Xiang* (《左傳•
襄公二十六年》).

Source: 中央研究院《搜詞尋字》.

(474) "祥" here is "ominous omens (凶的徵兆)", as in:

    I.   "亳有祥, 桑、穀共生于朝. 孔穎達 《正義》 : 祥是惡事先見之徵" in the *Book of Documents - Common Possession of Pure Virtue* (《書經•咸有一德》). See 《重編國語辭典修訂本》.

    II. "妖孽自外來謂之祥" in the *Book of Han - Treatise on the Five Elements* (《漢書•五行志》). See *Kangxi Dictionary* (《康熙字典》).

    Note "祥" does mean "fortuitous and ominous omens (吉凶之兆)". See *Kangxi Dictionary* (《康熙字典》). In our context, however, it should be interpreted as "ominous omens" only.

(475) "使氣" here is "headstrong and assertive (恣逞意氣)", as in Su E's (蘇鶚) *Du Yang Za Bian* (《杜陽雜編》) : "魚朝恩專權使氣, 公卿不敢仰視." See 《漢語大詞典》.

(476) See footnote 256.

(477) See footnote 261 and Chapter 30 Line 91.

(478) See footnote 262.

(479) See Chapter 30 Line 91.

(480) This is because Tao cannot be described in words. See Chapter 1 Line 1.

(481) See footnote 435.

(482) "分" here is "chaos (紛亂貌)", as in *Gui Gu Zi - Di Xi* (《鬼谷子•抵巇》): "天下分錯." See 中央研究院 《搜詞尋字》.
    See also Chapter 4 Line 11.

(483) "以" here is "rely on". See footnote 165.

(484) "正" here is "proper (合規範/合標準)", as in *The Analects - Zi Han* (《論語•子罕》): "吾自衛反魯, 然後樂正, 《雅》、《頌》各得其所." See 中央研究院《搜詞尋字》.

(485) "以" here is "consider (認為/以為)", as in
  I.   "以, 猶謂也" in *The Book of Expletives* (《經傳釋詞》).
  II. "告臧孫, 臧孫以難; 告郈孫, 郈孫以可" in *The Commentary of Zuo - the Twenty-fifth Year of Duke Zhao* (《左傳•昭公二十五年》).
  III. "人人自以得上意" in the *Book of Han - Annals of Emperor Yuan* (《漢書•元帝紀》).
  Source: 中央研究院《搜詞尋字》.

(486) "奇" here means "evil and ominous (奇邪/詭異不正)", as in Liu Zongyuan's (柳宗元) *Shi Ling Lun Xia* (《時令論下》) : "必言其中正, 而去其奇袞." See 中央研究院《搜詞尋字》.
  Accordingly, employing troops is a sign of bad omen (兵者不祥之器). See Chapter 31 Line 92.

(487) See footnote 405.

(488) See Chapter 48 Line 133 and footnote 406.

(489) The correct interpretation in vernacular Chinese of "以正治國, 以奇用兵, 以無事取天下" should be:
  "治國依仗正道, 用兵認為不祥, 治天下憑藉不做大事."
  (interpreted by Kwok Kin Poon)

(490) This corresponds to "when one aims to accomplish anything great, one is unqualified to rule all under Heaven (及其有事, 不足以取天下)" in Chapter 48 Line 133.

(491) "利器" here refers to "instruments that benefit people individually", such as currency, trade, and other social policies.

(492) "滋" here means "increasing (增長)", as indicated in
Shuowen Jiezi (《說文解字》): "滋, 益也."

(493) "昏" here means "chaos (亂)", as in the *Book of Documents - Speech at Mu* (《書經•牧誓》): "昏棄厥肆祀弗答. 傳:
昏, 亂也. 疏: 昏闇於事必亂, 故昏爲亂也." See *Kangxi Dictionary*
(《康熙字典》).

(494) The correct interpretation in vernacular Chinese of "民多利
器, 國家滋昏" should be:
> "百姓得到更多有利自己的工具(例如貨幣、貿易等), 國家便
> 益增混亂了."
> (interpreted by Kwok Kin Poon)

(495) See footnote 314.

(496) See Chapter 48 Line 133 and footnote 406.

(497) See footnote 148.

(498) "淳淳" here means "simple and honest (淳樸篤厚)", as in
Zhang Shao's (張紹) *Chong You Guan* (《沖佑觀》): "皇風蕩蕩,
黔首淳淳." See 《重編國語辭典修訂本》.

(499) "察察" here is "tactful and discerning (分別辨析)", as in the
New Book of Tang - Biography of Tutu Chengcui (《新唐書•吐突
承璀傳》): "以黃門直東宮, 為掖廷局博士, 察察有才." See 《重
編國語辭典修訂本》.

(500) "缺缺" here means "slick and cunning (詐僞貌/具小聰明
的)", as in Liu Zongyuan's (柳宗元) *Tong Ye Feng Di Bian*
(《桐葉封弟辨》): "是直小丈夫缺缺者之事, 非周公所宜用, 故不
可信." See 《重編國語辭典修訂本》.

(501) "極" here means "ultimate (頂點)" as indicated in *Shuowen*

Jiezi Zhu (《說文解字注》) : "極, 凡至高至遠皆謂之極."

(502) "正" here should be interpreted as "good/agreeable (完善/美好)", as in *Yili - Shi Guan Li* (《儀禮•士冠禮》) : "三加曰, 以歲之正, 以月之令, 咸加爾服. 鄭玄注 : 正, 猶善也." See 中央研究院《搜詞尋字》.

(503) The correct interpretation in vernacular Chinese of "孰知其極？ 其無正" should be:
> "誰曉得這禍這福最終會是怎麼樣呢? 這實在沒有所謂美善的呀!"
> (interpreted by Kwok Kin Poon)

(504) See footnote 486.

(505) "方" here is "duly (正直)", as in the *Book of Han - Biography of Dong Zhongshu* (《漢書•董仲舒傳》) : "悼王道之不昭, 故舉賢良方正之士." See 《重編國語辭典修訂本》.

(506) See footnote 237.

(507) "廉" here means "uncorrupted with integrity (廉潔)", as in:
I. "廉, 清也" in *Yupian* 《玉篇•闈部》.
II. "貧者見廉, 富者見義" in *Mo Yze - Xiushen* (《墨子•修身》).
Source: 中央研究院《搜詞尋字》.

(508) "劌" here means "hurt (傷)", as in Yu Ji's (虞集) *Yue Sheng Tang Ji* (《悅生堂記》) : "內劌其心, 外伐其形." See 《重編國語辭典修訂本》.

(509) "直" here means "honestly (正直)", as in *The Commentary of Zuo - the Twenty-eighth Year of Duke Xi* (《左傳•僖公二十八年》) : "師直為壯, 曲為老." See 《重編國語辭典修訂本》.

(510) "肆" here means "conflict (衝突)", as in *The Book of Odes*

- *Greater Odes of the Kingdom - Huang Yi* (《詩經•大雅•皇矣》) : "是伐是肆, 是絕是忽. 鄭玄箋 : 肆, 犯突也." See 中央研究院《搜詞尋字》.

(511) "治" here means "cultivate (修養)", as in:
    I.   "仁者之思也恭，聖人之思也樂，此治心之道也" in *Xun-zi - Jiebi* (《荀子•解蔽》).
    II. "或問治己. 曰：治己以仲尼" in *Fayan - XiuShen* (《法言•修身》).
    Source: 中央研究院《搜詞尋字》.
  "人" here means "self (自己)", as in *Nineteen Old Poems -Marching On and On* (《古詩十九首•行行重行行》) : "思君令人老，歲月忽已晚." See 中央研究院《搜詞尋字》.

(512) "事" here means "to pursue/serve (奉行/從事)", as in *Han-feitzu - Nan Yi* (《韓非子•難一》): "今管仲不務尊主明法, 而事增寵益爵." See 《漢語大字典》.

(513) "嗇" here is "farmer (農夫)", as in:
    I.   "嗇, 農人" by Wang Bi (王弼). See 王弼《老子王弼注》. 台北: 新興書局, 1964, p.071.
    II. "田夫謂之嗇夫" in *Shuowen Jiezi Zhu* (《說文解字注》).

(514) "德" here is not "virtue" but is "attainment/yield (得)", as in:
    I.   "德, 得也" in *Guangya - Shigu III* (《廣雅•釋詁三》).
    II. "是故用財不費, 民德不勞, 其興利多矣. 孫詒讓《閒詁》: 德與得通" in *Mo Yze - Economy of Expenditures I* (《墨子•節用上》).
    Source: 中央研究院《搜詞尋字》.
  Wang Bi (王弼) further annotated:
    "唯重積德不欲銳速, 然後乃能使早服其常, 故曰早服謂之重積德者也."
    "It is solely because the farmer focuses on amassing yield without the desire to rush that the farmer can obey

Nature from the very beginning. Hence, this is why 'Having obeyed Nature from the very beginning can be called as focusing on gradually amassing one's yield'."
(interpreted by KS Vincent Poon)
Source: 王弼《老子王弼注》. 台北: 新興書局, 1964, p.072.

"Without the desire to rush" and "gradually" are important, for "the most magnificent worldly entity evolves gradually and requires a long time to become established (大器晚成)". See Chapter 41 Line 117.

(515) "克" here means "competent (勝任)", as in *Shuowen Jiezi* (《說文解字》): " 克, 肩也. 徐鍇曰 : 肩, 任也. 負何之名也. 與人肩膊之義通, 能勝此物謂之克."

(516) "極" here means "limit (盡頭)", as in:
  I.   "極, 已也" in *Guangya - Shigu IV* (《廣雅•釋詁四》).
  II. "極, 終也" in *Guangyun* (《廣韻•職韻》).
  III. "悠悠蒼天, 曷其有極. 鄭玄箋 : 極, 已也" in *The Book of Odes - Odes Of Tang - Bao Yu* (《詩經•唐風•鴇羽》).
  Source: 中央研究院《搜詞尋字》.

Why is it that "there is no task in which one is not competent" and "one's limit cannot be known"? If one obeys Nature from the very beginning, then one is with the limitless Tao. As Wang Bi (王弼) annotated here:
  "道無窮也."
  Source: 王弼《老子王弼注》. 台北: 新興書局, 1964, p.072.

(517) The correct interpretation in vernacular Chinese of Line 160 should be:
  "在修養自己事奉大自然的事情上, 大家就比不上農夫了. 祇有農夫, 才可稱做起初就已服從了大自然(德). 起初就已服從大自然, 乃可稱之為重視慢慢累積而得到收穫. 能重視

慢慢累積而得成果, 那就無所不能勝任了. 無所不能勝任,
人們便不知道你能力的極限了."

(interpreted by Kwok Kin Poon)

(518) "有" is "為", as in:

I. "有, 猶為也. 為、有一聲之轉, 故為可訓為有, 有亦可訓
為" in *The Book of Expletives* (《經傳釋詞》).

II. "眇能視, 不足以有明也" in the *Book of Changes - Lu* (
《易經•履》).

Source: 中央研究院《搜詞尋字》.

This "為" means "rule (治理)", as in:

I. "為, 治也" in *Xiao Erya - Expanding Old Words* (《小
爾雅•廣詁》).

II. "為政以德" in *The Analects - Wei Zheng* (《論語•為
政》).

Source: 中央研究院《搜詞尋字》.

(519) "之" here is "apply (用)", as in *Strategies of the Warring
States - Strategies of Qi III* (《戰國策•齊策三》): "故物舍其所
長, 之其所短, 堯亦有所不及矣. 高誘注：之, 猶用也." See 中央研
究院《搜詞尋字》.

(520) "母" here is "motherly root of all (根源)", as in *Huainanzi -
Chu Zhen* (《淮南子•俶真》): "涅非緇也, 青非藍也. 茲雖遇其
母, 而無能復化已. 高誘注：母, 本也." See 中央研究院《搜詞尋
字》.

Accordingly, in our context, this "母" can then be interpreted
as "motherly Nature" or even "Manifestation of Tao (德)". See
Chapter 1 Line 1.

(521) The correct interpretation in vernacular Chinese of "莫知其
極, 可以有國. 有國之母, 可以長久" should be:

"人們不知道你能力的極限, 你便可以治理國家了. 用德來
治理國家, 那就可以長久了."

(interpreted by Kwok Kin Poon)

(522) "長生久視" here means "長生久活", as in *Master Lu's Spring and Autumn Annals - Zhong Ji* (《呂氏春秋•重己》 : "世之人主貴人, 無賢不肖, 莫不欲長生久視. 高誘注 : 視, 活也." See 《漢語大詞典》.

(523) Why should one be as mindful as cooking a small fish in governing? Laozi had always cherished the benefit of allowing Tao to act naturally with no human interference. Such is like cooking a small fish: avoid meddling for the best result. As such, Wang Bi (王弼) annotated:

> "不擾也, 躁則多害, 靜則全真."
> "Do not disturb, for rashness delivers much harm, while tranquillity bears the full nature of all things."
> (interpreted by KS Vincent Poon)
> Source: 王弼《老子王弼注》. 台北: 新興書局, 1964, p.072.

(524) "莅" here means "govern (治理)", as in *Mengzi - Liang Hui Wang I* (《孟子•梁惠王上》): "莅中國而撫四夷也." See 《漢語大字典》.

(525) "鬼" here means "wit (敏慧)", as in:

I. "虔、儇, 慧也...自關而東, 趙、魏之間謂之黠, 或謂之鬼" in *Fangyan - Volume I* (《方言•卷一》).

II. "鬼, 慧也" in *Guangya - Shigu I* (《廣雅•釋詁一》).

Source: 中央研究院《搜詞尋字》.

(526) "亦" here means "surely (確實)", as in the *Book of the Later Han - Elaboration on Biography of Dou Rong* (《後漢書•竇融傳贊》) : "悃悃安豐, 亦稱才雄. 李賢注 : 亦, 猶實也." See 中央研究院《搜詞尋字》.

(527) For Line 162, many incorrectly took "鬼" as "ghosts" or "evil spirits" and "神" as "gods" or "deities". Laozi had only asked one to follow Tao and had never addressed the existence

of supernatural entities.

"Ghosts" or "Deities" may be consistent with some branches of Taoist religion (道教), but these are certainly not consistent with *Tao Te Ching*, the canon of Taoism (道家).

Wise sages inherently do not harm anyone, for they follow Tao, which benefits all without doing any harm (Chapter 81 Line 219: "天之道, 利而不害").

The correct interpretation in vernacular Chinese of Line 162 should be:

"治理大國如烹煮小魚(務必留神, 切勿傷害魚身的完好). 用道來治理天下的人, 他的敏慧不會是他的精神. 並不是因為他的敏慧不是他的精神, 而是他的精神不會傷害人. 並不是因為他的精神不傷害人, 而是遵道的聖人確實本來就是不會傷害人啊!"

(interpreted by Kwok Kin Poon)

(528) "交" here means "come together (俱/共)", as in:
  I. "交, 俱也" in *Xiao Erya - Guang Yan* (《小爾雅•廣言》).
  II. "交, 共也" in *Yupian* (《玉篇•交部》).
  Source: 中央研究院《搜詞尋字》.

(529) See footnote 528. If a great and powerful state humbles itself to a lowly position, it will then be able to draw everyone to it. Hence, all shall come together, as Wang Bi (王弼) annotated:
  "天下所歸會也."
  Source: 王弼《老子王弼注》. 台北: 新興書局, 1964, p.073.

(530) "取" here means "acceptance (接受)", as in:
  I. "取, 受也" in *Guangyun* (《廣韻•麌韻》).
  II. "取衣者亦以篋. 鄭玄注: 取, 猶受也" in *The Classic of Rites - Sang Da Ji* (《禮記•喪大記》).
  Source: 中央研究院《搜詞尋字》.

(531) "或" here is "is/are/have (有)", as in:

    I.   "或, 有也" in *Guangya - Shigu I* (《廣雅•釋詁一》).

    II.   "有一於此, 未或不亡" in the *Book of Documents - Songs of the Five Sons* (《書經•五子之歌》).

    Source: 中央研究院《搜詞尋字》.

(532) The correct interpretation in vernacular Chinese of Line 165 should be:

"故此, 大國若以謙下來對待小國, 則取得小國的信服; 小國以謙下來接待大國, 則取得大國的信任。所以, 他們有些憑謙下以取得信服, 有些憑謙下而取得信任."

(interpreted by Kwok Kin Poon)

(533) "兼畜" here means "subjugate (兼并/并吞)". See《漢語大詞典》.

(534) "入" here means "adopt (采納)", as in:

    I.   "入, 納也" in *Yupian* (《玉篇》).

    II.   "諫而不入, 則莫之繼也" in *The Commentary of Zuo - the Second Year of Duke Xuan* (《左傳•宣公二年》).

    Source: 中央研究院《搜詞尋字》.

(535) "事" here means "serve (侍奉)", as in:

    I.   "事, 奉也" in *Yupian* (《玉篇》).

    II.   "事父母, 能竭其力; 事君, 能致其身" in *The Analects - Xue Er* (《論語•學而》).

    Source: 中央研究院《搜詞尋字》.

(536) In "大者", "大" is "important (重要/重大)", as in Zhuge Liang's (諸葛亮) *Chu Shi Biao* (《出師表》): "故臨崩寄臣以大事也." See 《漢典》.

    "者" here is "an auxiliary word used at the end of a sentence as an intonation (語氣助詞)", as seen in *Mengzi - Li Lou II* (《孟子•離婁下》) : "大人者, 不失其赤子之心者也." See 中央研究院《搜詞尋字》.

(537) "奧" here is "a safe haven (庇蔭之所)", as indicated in *Zhengyun* (《正韻》): "奧, 室西南隅, 人所安息也." See *Kangxi Dictionary* (《康熙字典》).

"奧" here should not be taken as "deep" nor "mysterious", for Line 167 emphasizes that Tao is a safe haven for all.

(538) The correct interpretation in vernacular Chinese of "道者萬物之奧" should be:

"道是萬物安棲的地方."

(interpreted by Kwok Kin Poon)

(539) "保" here is "safeguard (安)", as in:
  I. "保, 定也" in *Guangya - Shigu IV* (《廣雅•釋詁四》).
  II. "保民而王, 莫之能禦也. 趙岐注：保, 安也" in *Mengzi - Liang Hui Wang I* (《孟子•梁惠王上》).
  Source: 中央研究院《搜詞尋字》.

(540) "尊" here is "according to (遵/依照)", as in *Mo Yze - Fortification of the City Gate* (《墨子•備城門》)："然則守者必善, 而君尊用之, 然後可以守也. 俞樾平議： 尊當為遵, 古字通也." See 中央研究院《搜詞尋字》.

(541) "加" here is "to gift and benefit others (施及/施加)", as in:
  I. "加, 施也" in *Zihui* (《字彙》).
  II. "此所謂勸賞不必遍加乎天下, 而天下從焉者也" in Han Yu's (韓愈) *Shang Zai Xiang Shu* (《上宰相書》).
  Source: 中央研究院《搜詞尋字》.

(542) In the Zhou era, "三公 (Three Chief Mentors)" refers to "the most honourable titles among all officials (人臣中最尊崇的三個官銜)", as in the *Book of Documents - Officers of Zhou* (《書經•周官》): "立太師、太傅、太保, 茲惟三公, 論道經邦, 燮理陰陽." See 《重編國語辭典修訂本》. Also see KS Vincent Poon and Kwok Kin Poon, *English Translation of Classical Chinese Calligraphy Masterpieces*, Cao Quan Stele, footnote 68, pp. 36-

37. Toronto: The SenSeis, 2019.

(543) "拱璧" here is "a grand piece of jade (大璧)", as in *The Commentary of Zuo - the Twenty-eighth Year of Duke Xiang* (《左傳•襄公二十八年》) : "與我其拱璧, 吾獻其柩. 孔穎達疏：拱, 謂合兩手也, 此璧兩手拱抱之, 故為大璧." See 《漢語大詞典》.

(544) "以" here is "have/carry (有)", as in:
I. "君之門以九重" in *Verses of Chu - Jiu Bian* (《楚辭•九辯》).
II. "今楚國雖小, 絕長續短, 猶以數千里, 豈特百里哉" in *Strategies of the Warring States - Strategies of Chu IV*(《戰國策•楚策四》).
Source: 中央研究院《搜詞尋字》.

(545) "先" here is "honour (尚/尊)", as in *Master Lu's Spring and Autumn Annals - Xian Ji* (《呂氏春秋•先己》): "五帝先道而後德. 高誘注: 先, 猶尚也." See 《漢語大字典》.

(546) "Four-horse carriages (駟馬)" refers to the high social status of a minister (including the Three Mentors), who had the privilege of having his carriage pulled by four horses (卿駕四). See footnote 340.

(547) "坐" here is "naturally (自然而然的)", as in:
I. "坐, 猶自也" in Zhang Xiang's (張相) *Annotations to Words and Phrases in Poems and Verses - Volume IV* (《詩詞曲語辭匯釋•卷四》).
II. "墮肢體黜聰明, 離形去知, 同於大通, 是謂坐忘" in *Zhuangzi - The Great and Most Honoured Master* (《莊子•大宗師》).
Source: 中央研究院《搜詞尋字》.

(548) "進" here is "progress to (行)", as in:
I. "進, 行也" in *Guangya - Shigu I* (《廣雅•釋詁一》).

II. "徒銜枚而進. 鄭玄注：進, 行也" in *The Rites of Zhou - Offices of Summer* (《周禮•夏官》).

III. "進而視之, 欲其微至也. 鄭玄注：進, 猶行也." in *Record of Trades - Lun Ren* (《考工記•輪人》).

Source: 中央研究院《搜詞尋字》.

(549) The correct interpretation in vernacular Chinese of Line 168 should be:

"對於不喜好道的人, 道又怎會丟棄他們呢？ 故此, 確立天子設置三公, 雖則天子有拱璧之大的財寶, 三公有駟馬之車的尊崇, 倒不如自然而然地實踐此道."

(interpreted by Kwok Kin Poon)

(550) "德" here is not Confucius's "moral virtue (德行)" nor "kindness". Since wise sages treat all people with no mercy (Chapter 5 Line 13: 聖人不仁, 以百姓為芻狗), they do not follow the human concept of having "good virtue (善德)" nor "kindness".

Wise sages merely manifest themselves by following Tao, which dictates that one reaps what one sows (Chapter 23 Line 71: "同於道者, 道亦樂得之; 同於德者, 德亦樂得之; 同於失者, 失亦樂得之"). Accordingly, wises sages respond with fair retribution and so will answer "enmity" with "enmity". Indeed, Tao excels in responding (Chapter 73 Line 197: "不言而善應").

As such, "報怨以德" here has nothing to do with Confucius's contention of "return kindness for injury (以德報怨)" seen in *The Classic of Rites - Biao Ji* (《禮記•表記》): "以德報怨, 則寬身之仁也." See James Legge's *The Sacred Books of China, The Texts of Confucianism*.

Many scholars of the past and present have mistakenly interpreted Laozi's "報怨以德" as Confucius's "以德報怨". One example is renowned late Qing scholar Kang Youwei (康有為), who wrote:

"以德報怨, 其學出於老子."

"Return kindness for injury; such thought is derived from Laozi."

(interpreted by KS Vincent Poon)

Source: *A Study of Confucius as a Reformer* (《孔子改制考》), 卷二, 周末諸子並起創教考之道家創教.

(551) The correct interpretation in vernacular Chinese of Line 170 should be:

"幹那沒有私慾的行為; 做那沒有大功的事情; 嚐那沒有好壞的味道. 無分大小多少, 我僅用大自然的規律(德)來回應仇怨."

(interpreted by Kwok Kin Poon)

(552) "作" here means "originate (始)", as in:
   I.   "作, 始也" in *Guangya - Shigu I* (《廣雅•釋詁一》).
   II. "烝民乃粒, 萬邦作乂" in the *Book of Documents - Yi and Ji* (《書經•益稷》).
   Source: 中央研究院《搜詞尋字》.

(553) "終" here is "ultimately (終究/畢竟)", as in:
   I.   "不矜細行，終累大德" in *Book of Documents - Lu Ao* (《書經• 旅獒》).
   II. "騰蛇乘霧，終為土灰" in Cao Cao's (曹操) *Steps through the Illustrious Gate - Gui Sui Shou* (《步出夏門行•龜雖壽》).
   Source: 中央研究院《搜詞尋字》.

(554) "安" here is "calm and tranquil (安靜)", as in:
   I.   "安, 靜也" in *Shuowen Jiezi* (《說文解字》).
   II. "君子安其身而後動. 孔穎達疏：故先須安靜其身而後動" in the *Book of Changes - The Great Treatise II* (《易經•繫辭下》).
   Source: 中央研究院《搜詞尋字》.

(555) "持" here is "grasp (掌握)", as in *Lunheng - Gu Xiang* (《論衡•骨相》)："君後三歲而入將相, 持國秉." See 中央研究院《搜詞尋字》.

(556) "兆" here is "begin/rise (開始)", as in *The Commentary of Zuo - the First Year of Duke Ai* (《左傳•哀公元年》) : " (少康) 能布其德, 而兆其謀, 以收夏眾, 撫其官職...遂滅過、戈, 復禹之績. 杜預注 : 兆, 始也." See 中央研究院《搜詞尋字》.

(557) "泮" here is "break apart (分開/分別)", as in *Records of the Grand Historian - Biography of Lu Jia* (《史記•陸賈傳》) : "自天地剖泮未始有也." See 《重編國語辭典修訂本》.

(558) "散" here means "break up (開裂)", as in:
  I. "淩澗尋我室, 散帙問所知" in Xie Lingyun's (謝靈運) *Chou Cong Di Hui Lian* (《酬從弟惠連》).
  II. "香草已堪回步履, 午風聊復散衣襟" in Wang Anshi's (王安石) *Ci Yu He Ji Cheng Bei Hui Shang Zhu You* (《次御河寄城北會上諸友》).
  Source: 中央研究院《搜詞尋字》.

(559) A sturdy tree (木) of one's entire embrace is not favourable, for "wood that is strong will be quickly chopped down (木強則兵)". See Chapter 76 Line 205.

(560) As such, one should not allow any sprout to rise in the first place.

(561) This "overly lavished elevated terrace (高臺)" is not favourable, for constructing too many luxurious buildings shall lead to ill-cultivated fields and empty granaries (朝甚除, 田甚蕪, 倉甚虛). See Chapter 53 Line 145.

(562) "起" here means "rises from (開始)", as in:
  I. "起, 引伸之為凡始事、凡興作之偁" in *Shuowen Jiezi Zhu* (《說文解字注》).
  II. "明法度, 定律令, 皆以始皇起" in *Records of the Grand Historian - Biography of Li Si* (《史記•李斯列傳》).
  Source: 中央研究院《搜詞尋字》.

(563) As such, one should not even accumulate any soil to build the terrace in the first place.

(564) This "journey (行/外遊)" of thousands of miles is not favourable, for as one walks further away from home and exhausts oneself, the less one knows about Tao (其出彌遠, 其知彌少). See Chapter 47 Line 130.

(565) "足下" here means "at one's foot (腳下)", as in Yue Fu Shi Ji - *Jiao Zhong Qing Qi* (《樂府詩集•焦仲卿妻》)："足下躡絲履, 頭上玳瑁光." See 《重編國語辭典修訂本》.

　　As such, one should not even make a single step to start any journey in the first place.

(566) The correct interpretation in vernacular Chinese of Line 173 should be:

　　　　"靜態的事情易於掌握, 未發生的事情易於謀策. 脆弱的事
　　　　情易於擊碎, 微小的事情易於破散. 在事情未發生前要預先
　　　　治理, 在事情未紛亂前要預先整治. 給人砍伐的粗如合抱的
　　　　巨樹, 生長自極細的幼苗; 甚費人力物力的九層巨大高臺,
　　　　開始於堆積第一筐的泥土; 令人疲累的千里外遊, 開始於你
　　　　提起腳掌走的第一步."
　　　　(interpreted by Kwok Kin Poon)

(567) "從" here means "conduct a matter (為/從事)", as in *Guan-zi - Zheng Shi* (《管子•正世》)："知得失之所在, 然後從事. 尹知章注：從, 為." See 中央研究院《搜詞尋字》.

(568) "過" here means "lost (失掉)", as in *Discourses of the States - Discourses of Zhou I* (《國語•周語上》)："夫天地之氣, 不失其序; 若過其序, 民亂之也. 韋昭注：過, 失也." See 中央研究院《搜詞尋字》.

　　In our context, this "lost" refers to the people losing their inherent simplicities bestowed by Tao while living in a sophisticated society.

(569) The correct interpretation in vernacular Chinese of "復衆人
之所過" should be:

"讓人們復得所失掉的道."

(interpreted by Kwok Kin Poon)

(570) "以" here is "merely (惟/衹)", as in *Strategies of the Warring States - Strategies of Qi IV* (《戰國策•齊策四》) : "君家所寡
有者, 以義耳." See 中央研究院《搜詞尋字》.

(571) "輔" here is "to facilitate (佐助)", as in:
I. "輔, 助也" in *Guangya - Shigu III* (《廣雅•釋詁二》).
II. "爾尚輔予一人" in the *Book of Documents - Speech of
Tang* (《書經•湯誓》).
Source: 中央研究院《搜詞尋字》.

(572) "以" here is "because (因為/由於)", as in *The Analects -
Wei Ling Gong* (《論語•衛靈公》) : "君子不以言舉人, 不以人廢
言." See 中央研究院《搜詞尋字》.

(573) "賊" here means "vandalize (毀)", as in:
I. "賊, 敗也. 段玉裁注：敗者, 毀也. 毀者, 缺也" in
Shuowen Jiezi Zhu (《說文解字注》).
II. "毀則為賊. 杜預注：毀則, 壞法也" in *The Commen-
tary of Zuo - the Eighteenth Year of Duke Wen* (《左傳
•文公十八年》).
Source: 中央研究院《搜詞尋字》.

(574) "稽" here means "the same (同)", as annotated by Wang
Bi (王弼): "稽, 同也."See王弼《老子王弼注》. 台北: 新興書局,
1964, p.079.

(575) "與" here is "engage in (參與)", as in:
I. "與, 參與也" in *Guangyun* (《廣韻•御韻》).
II. "非天下之至變, 其孰能與於此" in the *Book of Chang-
es - The Great Treatise I* (《易經•繫辭上》).

Source: 中央研究院《搜詞尋字》.

(576) See footnote 114

(577) "言" here is "oneself (我)", as in:
    I.   "言，我也" in *Erya - Shigu I* (《爾雅•釋詁上》).
    II. "彤弓弨兮，受言藏之. 毛傳：言，我也" in *The Book of Odes - Minor Odes of the Kingdom - Tong Gong* (《詩經•小雅•彤弓》).
    III. "弋言加之，與子宜之. 鄭玄箋：言，我也" in *The Book of Odes - Odes Of Zheng - NueYue Ji Ming* (《詩經•鄭風•女曰雞鳴》).
    Source: 中央研究院《搜詞尋字》.

(578) The correct interpretation in vernacular Chinese of "是以欲上民, 必以言下之" should be:
    "故此, 若想居於百姓之上, 那就必須我先處於百姓之下."
    (interpreted by Kwok Kin Poon)

(579) "先" here is "lead (引導/倡導)", as in:
    I.   "明智禮, 足以教之, 上身服以先之. 尹知章注：所以率先於下也" in *Guanzi - Da Kuang* (《管子•權修》).
    II. "躬以簡儉為天下先" in Wang Anshi's (王安石) *Ben Chao Bai Nian Wu Shi Zha Zi* (《本朝百年無事札子》).
    Source: 中央研究院《搜詞尋字》.

(580) "重" here is "burdensome (負累)", as in *The Book of Odes - Minor Odes of the Kingdom - Wu Jiang Da Che* (《詩經•小雅•無將大車》)："無思百憂, 祇自重兮. 鄭玄箋：重, 猶累也." See 中央研究院《搜詞尋字》.

(581) The correct interpretation in vernacular Chinese of "是以聖人處上而民不重, 處前而民不害" should be:
    "故此聖人居於高位而百姓不覺得他是一重負擔, 居於領導而百姓也不覺得他會帶來傷害."
(interpreted by Kwok Kin Poon)

(582) "樂推" here means "willing to endorse (樂意擁戴)", as in the *Book of Song - Annals of Emperor Wu II* (《宋書•武帝紀中》) : "自非百姓樂推, 天命攸集, 豈伊在予, 所得獨專." See 《漢語大詞典》.

(583) Tao is indescribable (Chapter 1 Line 1), for it is infinitely great without limit. If an entity can be described by humans and appears as great, it must thus be describable and so cannot be infinitely great without limit. Hence, it must be small, as Wang Bi (王弼) annotated:
> "肖則失其所以為大矣."
> Source: 王弼《老子王弼注》. 台北: 新興書局, 1964, p.080.

The correct interpretation in vernacular Chinese of Line 181 should be:
> "世人都認為我說道大, 但它卻全不似大. 正因為大, 故此它才全不似大呢. 假若似大, 它老早就是細啦!"
> (interpreted by Kwok Kin Poon)

(584) "持" here means "uphold (握住)", as in:
I.   "持, 握也" in *Shuowen Jiezi* (《說文解字》).
II. "媼之送燕后也, 持其踵為之泣" in *Strategies of the Warring States - Strategies of Zhao IV* (《戰國策•趙策四》).
Source: 中央研究院《搜詞尋字》.

(585) "保" here is "rely on (恃/憑藉)", as in *The Commentary of Zuo - the Twenty-third Year of Duke Xi* (《左傳•僖公二十三年》) : "保君父之命而享其生祿, 於是乎得人. 杜預注 : 保, 猶恃也." See中央研究院《搜詞尋字》.

(586) "慈" here is "earnest adoration (篤愛)", as in *The Com-

mentary of Zuo - the Twenty-seventh year of Duke Zhuang (《左傳•莊公二十七年》) : "夫禮樂慈愛, 戰所畜也. 孔穎達疏：慈謂愛之深也." See中央研究院《搜詞尋字》.

"慈" here is not Confucius's "benevolence and kindness (仁慈)". This is because wise sages do not follow the concept of being benevolent or having kindness (Chapter 5 Line 13: 聖人不仁, 以百姓為芻狗).

Accordingly, "慈" only applies to a wise sage's attitude towards Tao, which is "earnest adoration".

(587) "儉" here is "frugality (節省/簡樸)", as in:
I.   "儉, 省節也" in Pianhai Leibian (《篇海類編•人物類•人部》).
II. "禮, 與其奢也, 寧儉. 皇侃注：去奢從約謂之儉" in The Analects - Ba Yi (《論語•八佾》).
Source: 中央研究院《搜詞尋字》.

(588) See footnote 579.

(589) Why should one dare not to lead and be the most preeminent? This is because "if one wishes to be positioned above the people, then one must put oneself below the people". See Chapter 69 Line 179.

(590) The correct interpretation in vernacular Chinese of "我有三寶, 持而保之: 一曰慈, 二曰儉, 三曰不敢為天下先" should be:
"我有三寶, 常緊握而依仗著它: 一稱為篤愛於道, 二稱為節儉素樸, 三稱為不敢做天下的領導."
(interpreted by Kwok Kin Poon)

(591) "廣" here means "prosper (增多/增強)", as in the Book of Han - Treatise on Food and Money I (《漢書•食貨志上》) : "薄賦斂, 廣畜積." See 中央研究院《搜詞尋字》.

(592) "且" here means "adopt (取)", as annotated by Wang Bi (

王弼): "且, 猶取也." See 王弼《老子王弼注》. 台北: 新興書局, 1964, p.081.

(593) See footnote 313.

(594) See Chapter 28 Line 80 and footnote 221.

(595) See footnote 104.

(596) "士" here means "the commander-in-chief of soldiers (帥)", as annotated by Wang Bi (王弼): "士, 卒之帥也." See 王弼《老子王弼注》. 台北: 新興書局, 1964, p.081.

(597) "與" here means "to battle (戰)", as in *The Commentary of Zuo - the Ninth year of Duke Ai* (《左傳•哀公九年》) : "宋方吉, 不可與也. 杜預注：不可與戰." See 中央研究院《搜詞尋字》.

(598) See footnote 408.

(599) See Chapter 66 Line 180.

(600) See footnote 325.

(601) "扔" here means "defeat (摧)", as in the *Book of the Later Han - Biography of Ma Rong* (《後漢書•馬融》): "竄伏扔輪. 註: 言爲輪所摧也." See *Kangxi Dictionary* (《康熙字典》).

(602) "無敵" here means "being defeated (不敵)", for "無" can be "不" according to *Kangxi Dictionary* (《康熙字典》): "無, 猶不也."

(603) Line 187 does not mean Laozi had recommended one to be pretending, scheming, or calculating. Rather, Laozi here advised one should always be cautious and consider oneself to be at a disadvantage. See Line 188.

(604) "幾" here means "will then (則)" as in:

  I. "幾, 猶則也" in *A Collection of the Annotations of Functional Words in Ancient Books - Volume V* (《古書虛字集釋•卷五》).

  II. "其無乃廢先王之訓, 而王幾頓乎" in *Discourses of the States - Discourses of Zhou I* (《國語•周語上》).

  Source: 中央研究院《搜詞尋字》.

(605) For Laozi's treasures (寶), see Chapter 67 Line 182.

(606) "抗" here means "raises (舉)", as in:

  I. "抗, 舉也" in *Guangya - Shigu I* (《廣雅•釋詁一》).

  II. "大侯既抗, 弓矢斯張. 毛傳: 抗, 舉也" in *The Book of Odes - Minor Odes of the Kingdom - Bin Zhi Chu Yan* (《詩經•小雅•賓之初筵》).

  Source: 中央研究院《搜詞尋字》.

(607) "加" here is "to counter an enemy (抵擋敵人)", as in:

  I. "加, 當也" in 王弼《老子王弼注》. 台北: 新興書局, 1964, p.082.

  II. "當, 敵也" in *Yupian* (《玉篇》). See 中央研究院《搜詞尋字》.

  III. "然則君請當其君, 臣請當其臣. 何休注：當, 猶敵也" in *Gongyang Zhuan - the Twenty-third Year of Duke Zhuang* (《公羊傳•莊公十三年》). See 中央研究院《搜詞尋字》.

(608) The sorrowful side considers itself to be at a disadvantage and so never underestimates its enemies. Hence, it is more likely to prevail.

(609) Why most are unable to understand and carry out Laozi's words? This is because many are tainted with selfish desires and lusts for glory, as annotated by Wang Bi (王弼):

  "惑於躁欲, 故曰莫之能知也; 迷於榮利, 故曰莫之能行也."

Source: 王弼《老子王弼注》. 台北: 新興書局, 1964, p.083.

(610) "言" here means "narratives (言論/見解)", as in:

    I.   "如何昊天？辟言不信" in *The Book of Odes - Minor Odes of the Kingdom - Yu Wu Zheng* (《詩經•小雅•雨無正》).

    II. "言無二貴, 法不兩適. 故言行而不軌於法令者必禁" in *Hanfeitzu - Wen Bian* (《韓非子•問辯》).

Source: 中央研究院《搜詞尋字》.

(611) "宗" here means "foundational basis (根本)", as in:

    I.   "宗, 本也" in *Guangya - Shigu III* (《廣雅•釋詁三》).

    II. "禮賓矜窮, 禮之宗也. 韋昭注：宗, 本也" in *Discourses of the States - Discourses of Jin* IV (《國語•晉語四》).

Source: 中央研究院《搜詞尋字》.

(612) See footnote 208. The "lord (君)" here refers to Manifestation of Tao.

(613) The correct interpretation in vernacular Chinese of Line 190 should be:

"言論要有個根本, 事物總有個主宰(德). 祇因人們不懂得這道理, 所以才不了解我."

(interpreted by Kwok Kin Poon)

(614) "希" here is "rare (罕/少)", as in *Erya - Shigu II* (《爾雅•釋詁下》)："希, 罕也." See 中央研究院《搜詞尋字》.

(615) "則" here is "model after (效法)", as in:

    I.   "惟天為大, 惟堯則之" in *Mengzi - Teng Wen Gong I* (《孟子•滕文公上》).

    II. "皋陶於是敬禹之德, 令民皆則禹" in *Records of the Grand Historian - Annals of Xia* (《史記•夏本紀》).

Source: 中央研究院《搜詞尋字》.

(616) The correct interpretation in vernacular Chinese of Line 191 should be:

"了解我的人極少, 效法我的更屬難能可貴. 故此也證明了
聖人身上穿的是卑賤的麻衣, 心內藏的卻是無價的寶玉呀!"

(interpreted by Kwok Kin Poon)

(617) "知不知, 上" should not be taken as "understand yet pretend not to understand is superior". This is because Laozi had always opposed dishonesty.

"知不知, 上" should also not be taken as "understand that one does not understand is superior". Even those who follow and understand Tao can only be considered as enlightened, not superior. Merely understanding that one does not understand Tao certainly does not qualified to be called superior.

Line 192 should be interpreted along with the previous "知我者希" in Line 191. This "知" in Line 192 "知不知, 上" carries the same implication of understanding Laozi "知我" in Line 191.

Remarkably, Laozi's teaching of "understanding (知)" and "not understanding (不知)" was nicely borrowed by Tang Calligrapher Sun Guoting (孫過庭) in his *A Narrative on Calligraphy* (書譜):

"門生獲書機, 父削而子懊. 知與不知也. 夫士屈于不知己,
而申於知己. 彼不知也, 曷足怪乎?! ... 老子云: '下士聞
道, 大咲之; 不咲之則不足以為道也.'"

"...the story of a disciple (of Wang Xizhi) who first acquired Wang Xizhi's calligraphy scribed on his long table but later lost it for his father scraped it off, leaving the son shocked and remorseful. Such stories illustrate the difference between truly comprehending and not comprehending the art. Alas, an intellect grieves when others do not comprehend him and becomes free and at ease when others comprehend him. For those who do not comprehend, why should we bother to blame or criticize

them?! ... as Laozi once stated, 'Scholars of the lowest class, when they have heard about Dao, laugh greatly at it. If it were not (thus) laughed at, it would not be fit to be the Dao.'"
Source: KS Vincent Poon & Kwok Kin Poon, *A Narrative on Calligraphy by Sun Guoting, Revised and Enhanced Edition* 英譯書譜增訂版, pp.61-62.

(618) "病" here is "suffering from exhaustion (苦/疲憊)", as in:

    I.   "人極于病. 傳: 欲使惡人極于病苦, 莫敢犯者" in the *Book of Documents - Marquis of Lu on Punishments* (《書經•呂刑》). See *Kangxi Dictionary* (《康熙字典》).

    II. "今日病矣, 予助苗長矣！趙岐注：病, 罷也" in *Mengzi - Gong Sun Chou I* (《孟子•公孫丑上》). See 中央研究院《搜詞尋字》.

    III. "此恐吾攻己, 故示我不病. 請為轂千乘, 卒三萬, 與分吳地也" in *Shuo Yuan - Quan Mou* (《說苑•權謀》).

    Source: 中央研究院《搜詞尋字》.

  "病" here cannot be "diseased" nor "sick". All humans, including those who understand Tao, can contract diseases and become sick.

(619) The correct interpretation in vernacular Chinese of Line 192 should be:

"能知曉那些不懂道的, 此乃優尚; 沒能知曉那懂道的, 可就疲苦了."
(interpreted by Kwok Kin Poon)

(620) The correct interpretation in vernacular Chinese of Line 193 should be:

"因為了解疲苦之所以成為疲苦, 所以才會不疲苦. 聖人不疲苦, 因為他了解疲苦之所以成為疲苦, 所以就不疲苦了."
(interpreted by Kwok Kin Poon)

(621) "狎" here means "alter (易)", as in *Yupian* (《玉篇》): "狎, 易也." See *Kangxi Dictionary* (《康熙字典》).

(622) "厭" here means "inflict harm (損害/迫害)", as in *The Commentary of Zuo - the Second Year of Duke Wen* (《左傳•文公二年》): "及晉處父盟以厭之. 註: 厭猶損也." See *Kangxi Dictionary* (《康熙字典》).

(623) The correct interpretation in vernacular Chinese of Line 194 should be:

> "當百姓再不懼怕君主的威嚇時, 他們天大的怒威便即來臨
> 了. 不要遷移人們居住的地方, 也不要傷害人們維生的生
> 計. 因為你不迫害百姓, 故此百姓才不會傷害你."
> (interpreted by Kwok Kin Poon)

(624) "自知" here means "understand oneself (了解自身)", as in Su Shi's (蘇軾) *Yu Ye Jin Shu Shu* 《與葉進叔書》: "僕聞有自知之明者, 乃所以知人." See 《重編國語辭典修訂本》. See also Chapter 33 Line 98.

(625) "敢" here means "aggressive (進取)", as indicated in *Shuowen Jiezi* (《說文解字》).

(626) "殺" here means "caused to have an unnatural death (致死)" as in:

> I. "殺, 戮也" in *Shuowen Jiezi* (《說文解字》).
> II. "志士仁人, 無求生以害仁, 有殺身以成仁" in *The Analects - Wei Ling Gong* (《論語•衛靈公》).
> Source: 中央研究院《搜詞尋字》.

(627) The correct interpretation in vernacular Chinese of Line 196 should be:

> "勇於進取的那就喪命; 勇於不進取的那就活命. 這兩者, 有
> 利也有害. 大自然之所厭惡, 誰曉得箇中的原故呢? 所以就
> 聖人尚且覺得這是很困難的呀!"

(interpreted by Kwok Kin Poon)

(628) "繂" here is "at ease (舒緩/舒坦)", as indicated in *Shuowen Jiezi* (《說文解字》): "繂, 帶緩也."

(629) "恢恢" here is "wide and far apart (寬闊廣大的樣子)", as in *Selections of Refined Literature - Lu Ji - Han Gao Zu Gong Chen Song* (《文選•陸機•漢高祖功臣頌》)："恢恢廣野, 誕節令圖." See 《重編國語辭典修訂本》.

(630) See footnote 486.

(631) "常" refers to Tao. See footnote 1.

(632) "司" here is "administrate (掌管/主持)", as in:
    I. "司, 主也. 盜賊司目, 民無所放" in *Guangya - Shigu III* (《廣雅•釋詁三》).
    II. "彼其之子, 邦之司直. 毛傳：司, 主也" in *The Book of Odes - Odes Of Zheng - Gao Qiu* (《詩經•鄭風•羔裘》).
    Source: 中央研究院《搜詞尋字》.

(633) The correct interpretation in vernacular Chinese of "常有司殺者殺. 夫代司殺者殺, 是謂代大匠斲" should be:
    "然而, 常道自有掌管殺戮的去殺. 你替代掌管殺戮的去殺, 這就叫做替代技藝高超的木匠來伐木了."
    (interpreted by Kwok Kin Poon)

(634) See footnote 614.

(635) See footnote 421.

(636) See footnote 365.

(637) "為" here means "seek (謀求)", as in *Mengzi - Jin Xin I* (《

孟子•盡心上》）：“雞鳴而起, 孳孳為利者, 跖之徒也.” See 中央研究院《搜詞尋字》.

(638) The correct interpretation in vernacular Chinese of Line 202 should be:

> “唯獨不貪求財物的君主, 才肯定遠勝那些視財如命、徵收重稅的君主哩!”

(interpreted by Kwok Kin Poon)

(639) “兵” here is “kill or inflict injury by a weapon (用兵器殺傷)”, as in *Records of the Grand Historian - Biography of Bo Yi* (《史記•伯夷列傳》)：“左右欲兵之.” See 中央研究院《搜詞尋字》.

In our context, since “兵” is applied to wood, it should be interpreted as “chop down by a tool”.

(640) “奉” here means “to gift to (送/給予)”, as in:
I.   “奉, 與也” in *Guangyun* (《廣韻•腫韻》).
II. “秦違蹇叔, 而以貪勤民, 天奉我也. 杜預注：奉, 與也” in *The Commentary of Zuo - the Thirty-third Year of Duke Xi* (《左傳•僖公三十三年》).
III. “比奉書, 即蒙寵答, 以感以怍” in Wang Anshi's (王安石) *Yu Ma Yun Pan Shu* (《與馬運判書》).
Source: 中央研究院《搜詞尋字》.

(641) “者” here is “an auxiliary word that is used at the end of a sentence as an intonation (語氣助詞)”. See footnote 536.

(642) Wise sages do not depend on others; they only rely on Tao. Tao also does not depend on others; it only relies on Tao itself. See footnote 13.

(643) “勝” here means “better than (優過之)”, as in *Master Zhou's Almanac* (《周子通書》): “實勝善也, 名勝恥也.” See *Kangxi Dictionary* (《康熙字典》).

(644) "以" here is "therefore (因此)", as in:

    I.   "以, 因也" in *Zhengzitong* (《正字通•人部》).

    II. "孝公得商君, 地以廣, 兵以強" in *Hanfeitzu - Jian Jie Shi Chen* (《韓非子•姦劫弒臣》).

    Source: 中央研究院《搜詞尋字》.

(645) "易" here is "replace (替代)", as in *The Commentary of Zuo - the Thirtieth Year of Duke Xi* (《左傳•僖公三十年》): "因人之力而敝之, 不仁; 失其所與, 不知; 以亂易整, 不武." See 中央研究院《搜詞尋字》.

(646) "受" here is "accept (容納)", as in:

    I.   "受, 容納也" in *Kangxi Dictionary* (《康熙字典》).

    II. "君子以虛受人" in the *Book of Changes - Xian* (《易經•咸》). See 中央研究院《搜詞尋字》.

(647) "垢" here is "shame (恥辱)", as in:

    I.   "國君含垢, 天之道也. 杜預注：忍垢恥" in *The Commentary of Zuo - the Fifteenth Year of Duke Xuan* (《左傳•宣公十五年》). See《漢語大字典》.

    II. "忍垢苟全, 則犯詩人胡顏之譏" in *Selections of Refined Literature - Cao Zhi - Shang Ze Gong Ying Zhao Shi Biao* (《文選•曹植•上責躬應詔詩表》). See《重編國語辭典修訂本》.

(648) "社稷" originally means "god of the land and god of the crops (土神和穀神)", but later refers to "state (國)", as in:

    I.   "能執干戈以衛社稷, 雖欲勿殤也, 不亦可乎" in *The Classic of Rites - Tan Gong II* (《禮記•檀弓下》).

    II. "食人之祿, 當分人之憂, 苟利社稷, 死生以之" in Wang Shizhen's (王世貞) *Ming Feng Ji* (《鳴鳳記》).

    Source:《重編國語辭典修訂本》.

(649) "不祥" here means "misdeeds (不善)", as in *Strategies of the Warring States - Strategies of Qi IV* (《戰國策•齊策四》) : "

寡人不祥，被於宗廟之崇，沉於諂諛之臣." See《重編國語辭典修訂本》.

(650) "正言" here is "proper narratives (合於正道的言論)", as in Kuan Huan's (桓寬) *Yan Tie Lun* (《鹽鐵論》): "藥酒, 病之利也; 正言, 治之藥也." See《漢語大詞典》.

　　"言" is "言論", see footnote 610.

(651) "若" here is "is/are/does(乃)", not "seemingly" or "as if". See footnote 31.

(652) "正言若反" cannot be "proper narratives appear to be pointing towards the opposite" nor "proper narratives are seemingly improper". If these interpretations were true, then *Tao Te Ching* would have narrated "one should not follow Tao" in order to tell "one should follow Tao"; such is clearly not the case.

　　Tao embraces and includes all human points of views, for there is actually nothing that is absolutely agreeable nor disagreeable (Chapter 58 Line 158: "正復為奇, 善復為妖"). A wise ruler, therefore, merely focuses on returning all back to Tao by accepting the existence of countering ways manifested by Tao (Chapter 40 Line 115: 反者道之動). Such is the gist of Line 211.

　　Accordingly, the correct interpretation in vernacular Chinese of "正言若反" is:

　　　"合於正道的言論, 乃是容納一切相反面而同返於道的言論."

　　　(interpreted by Kwok Kin Poon)

　　Note "反" in "正言若反" can take the meaning of "countering ways", "restoring back to Tao", or both.

(653) "左契" here is "notes or documents that provide evidence of proof (證明文件/證明書)", such as "land deeds (田契)" or "contracts (契約)".

　　"左" carries the meaning of "evidence of proof (佐證/憑證)", as in:

　　　I.　"左, 證左也" in *Shiya - Shi Xun II* (《拾雅•釋訓中》).

II. "廷尉定國考問, 左驗明白. 顏師古注：左, 證左也. 言
當時在其左右見此事者也" in the *Book of Han - Biography of Yang Chang and Yang Jun* (《漢書•楊敞傳附
楊惲》).

Source: 中央研究院《搜詞尋字》.

"契" here is "notes or documents (券)", as in:

I. "契, 券也" in *Yupian* (《玉篇•大部》).

II. "掌稽市之書契. 鄭玄注：書契, 取予市物之券也" in
The Rites of Zhou - Offices of Earth (《周禮•地官》).

Source: 中央研究院《搜詞尋字》.

An example of "左契" as "notes or documents that provide
evidence of proof" can be seen in Du Mu's (杜牧) *Hang Zhou
Xin Zao Nan Ting Zi Ji* (《杭州新造南亭子記》)："今權歸於佛,
買福賣罪, 如持左契, 交手相付." See 《漢語大詞典》.

"Notes or documents that provide evidence of proof", such
as contracts, are generally made based upon willing mutual con-
sents. Accordingly, grievances can be minimized if all parties
follow these documents devotedly, as Wang Bi (王弼) annotated:

"左契防怨之所由生也."

Source: 王弼《老子王弼注》. 台北: 新興書局, 1964,
p.089.

(654) "責" here means "demand (索取)", as indicated in *Shuow-
en Jiezi* (《說文解字》): "責, 求也."

(655) "德" here is not Confucius's "moral virtues (德行)". Rather,
it is the resulting outcome (i.e., manifestation) of following Tao.
Laozi abhorred Confucius's "moral values". See Chapter 38
Line 108 and footnote 322.

(656) See footnote 632.

(657) "(契)" here refers to "documents that provide evidence of
proof (左契)". See footnote 653.

(658) "Che (徹)" here refers to "the land taxation system (田稅制度)" under Zhou Dynasty's Well-field system (井田制度), as elaborated in:

I. "徹, 稅也" in *Guangya - Shigu II* (《廣雅•釋詁二》).

II. "夏后氏五十而貢, 殷人七十而助, 周人百畝而徹, 其實皆什一也. 趙岐注：家耕百畝者徹, 取十畝以為賦. 名雖異而多少同, 故曰皆什一也" in *Mengzi - Teng Wen Gong I* (《孟子•滕文公上》).

III. "夫十一而稅, 周謂之徹" in the *Book of the Later Han - Biography of Lu Kang* (《後漢書•陸康傳》).

Source: 中央研究院《搜詞尋字》.

(659) Wise sages never demand anything from the people (Line 212: "不責於人"). Therefore, they only focus on adhering to agreements and documents (有德司契). Only those without the Manifestation of Tao will focus on demanding taxes from the people (無德司徹).

(660) "與" here means "support (助)", as in *Mengzi - Gong Sun Chou I* (《孟子•公孫丑上》): "取諸人以為善, 是與人為善者也. 朱熹集注：與, 猶助也." See 中央研究院《搜詞尋字》.

(661) "善" here should be distinguished from its usual meaning of "good", "nice", or "kind". Here, it refers to those who are "well-acquainted with Tao" or "rich in Tao". See footnote 35.

(662) The correct interpretation in vernacular Chinese of Line 213 should be:

"有德的人祇掌管田地約契, 無德的人掌管的是用稅制徹法來徵稅. 大自然之道可沒什麼親或不親的, 祇常常幫助那些喜好於道的人."

(interpreted by Kwok Kin Poon)

(663) "使" here is "makes/results in (讓/致使)", as in :

I. "維子之故, 使我不能餐兮" in *The Book of Odes -*

Odes Of Zheng - Jiao Tong (《詩經•鄭風•狡童》).

II. "出師未捷身先死, 長使英雄淚滿襟" in Du Fu's (杜甫) *Shu Xiang* (《蜀相》).

Source: 中央研究院《搜詞尋字》.

(664) "什伯" here means "more than a tenfold or a hundredfold (超過十倍百倍)", as in *Mengzi - Teng Wen Gong I* (《孟子•滕文公上》): "夫物之不齊, 物之情也. 或相倍蓰, 或相什伯, 或相千萬." See 《漢語大字典》.

(665) Why no contact with other states? This is because people living by Tao do not possess any selfish desire, and so all are content with whatever their circumstances. Accordingly, it is unnecessary to deal with any other state. Hence, Wang Bi (王弼) annotated these people as "having nothing to desire for themselves (無所欲求)". See 王弼《老子王弼注》. 台北: 新興書局, 1964, p.091.

(666) "既以" here is "since already (既然已經)", as in *Xunzi - Fu Guo* (《荀子•富國》) : "既以伐其本, 竭其原, 而焦天下矣." See 《漢語大詞典》.

(667) "為" here is "to gift (施/給與)", as in *The Commentary of Zuo - the Twenty-third Year of Duke Xiang* (《左傳•襄公二十三年》: "齊侯將為臧紇田. 杜預注:與之田邑." See 中央研究院《搜詞尋字》.

(668) Why do they possess plenty? Since wise sages gift themselves to all, everyone reveres and endorses them, as annotate by Wang Bi (王弼):

"物(人)所尊也."

Source: 王弼《老子王弼注》. 台北: 新興書局, 1964, p.091.

(669) "與" here means "bestow (給予)", as in:

I. "天子不能以天下與人" in *Mengzi - Wan Zhang I* (《孟

子・萬章上》).

 II. "此明君且常與, 而賢臣且常取也" in *Hanfeitzu - Zhong Xiao* (《韓非子・忠孝》).

 Source: 中央研究院《搜詞尋字》.

(670) Why are they more affluent? Since wise sages bestow themselves upon all, everyone follows them, as annotated by Wang Bi (王弼):

 "物所歸也."

 Source: 王弼《老子王弼注》. 台北: 新興書局, 1964, p.091.

(671) The correct interpretation in vernacular Chinese of Line 218 should be:

 "聖人不會為自己積聚財貨. 既然已經把自己的施予他人, 那麼自己就愈為富裕; 既然已經把自己的贈與他人, 那麼自己就愈為豐餘."

 (interpreted by Kwok Kin Poon)

(672) "利" is "benefit (利益)", as in:

 I. "利, 所得而喜也" in *Mo Yze - Canon I* (《墨子・經上》).

 II. "利, 害之反" in *Zhengzitong* (《正字通》).

 III. "是能容之, 以保我子孫黎民, 亦職有利哉" in the *Book of Documents - Tai Shi* (《書經・泰誓》).

 Source: 中央研究院《搜詞尋字》.

(673) "為" here should be "to gift (施)". See line 218 and footnote 667.

 "為" here should not be taken as "act", for "為而不爭" serves as a direct elaboration on "既以為人己愈有" in Line 218. Further, a wise sage focuses on "無為", not "為". See Chapter 2 Line 6.

(674) The correct interpretation in vernacular Chinese of Line 219 should be:

 "大自然之道, 乃利於萬物而不會傷害; 聖人之道, 是施與大眾而不會相爭."

 (interpreted by Kwok Kin Poon)

引用書目

English

Legge, James, *Sacred Books of the East,* Volume 27, *The Li king,* edited by Max Mueller. Oxford: Clarendon Press , 1885.

Legge, James, *Sacred Books of the East, The Texts of Taoism*, edited by Max Mueller. Oxford: Clarendon Press :1891.

Poon, KS Vincent & Poon, Kwok Kin, *A Narrative on Calligraphy by Sun Guoting, Revised and Enhanced Edition* 英譯書譜增訂版. Toronto: The SenSeis, 2019.

Poon, KS Vincent & Poon, Kwok Kin, *English Translation of Classical Chinese Calligraphy Masterpieces* 英譯法書. Toronto: The Senseis, 2019.

Poon, Kwok Kin, *A Collection of Kwok Kin Poon's Calligraphy* 潘國鍵書法集. Toronto: The Senseis, 2019.

Chinese

王弼,《老子王弼注》,華亭張氏本。台北: 新興書局, 1964。

朱熹,《四書集註》。香港: 太平書局 , 1968。

沈約,《宋書》。北京: 中華書局, 1974。

《易經》。鄭州: 中州古籍出版社, 1993。

河上公,《老子河上公注》,世德堂刊本。出版地及年代缺.

班固,《漢書》。香港: 中華書局, 1970。

高亨 ,《老子正詁》。上海: 開明書店, 1949。

康有為 ,《孔子改制考》。上海大同譯書局, 1897(?)。

張默生,《老子章句新釋》。上海:東方書社, 1946。

劉文典,《莊子補正》。雲南: 雲南人民出版社, 1980。

潘國鍵, 《 孫過庭書譜白話對譯 》 。多倫多: 尚尚齋, 2019 。

韓非, 《韓非子》。欽定四庫全書子部韓非子, 乾隆四十四年版。

Dictionary

段玉裁,《說文解字注》。臺北: 藝文印書館, 1966。

郭璞,《爾雅郭注》。台北: 新興書局, 1964。

《康熙字典》。上海: 上海書店, 1985。

《漢語大詞典》。上海: 上海辭書出版社, 2008。

《漢語大字典》。成都: 四川長江出版集團, 2010。

Websites

中央研究院,《搜詞尋字》。words.sinica.edu.tw/sou/sou.html。

中華民國教育部,《重編國語辭典修訂本》。dict.revised.moe.edu.tw/cbdic/。

國家教育研究院,《教育大辭書》。terms.naer.edu.tw/。

《漢典》。www.zdic.net。

The SenSeis

尚尚齋